W Thwaites

Our Convicts

Their riots and their causes: containing startling revelations of the frightful

abuses of our convict system, official correspondence, etc., etc.:

presented to Parliament

W Thwaites

Our Convicts

Their riots and their causes: containing startling revelations of the frightful abuses of our convict system, official correspondence, etc., etc.: presented to Parliament

ISBN/EAN: 9783337309374

Printed in Europe, USA, Canada, Australia, Japan

Cover: Foto ©ninafisch / pixelio.de

More available books at **www.hansebooks.com**

A BLUE BOOK.

OUR CONVICTS:

THEIR RIOTS AND THEIR CAUSES.

CONTAINING

STARTLING REVELATIONS

OF THE

FRIGHTFUL ABUSES OF OUR CONVICT SYSTEM.

OFFICIAL CORRESPONDENCE, ETC., ETC.,

PRESENTED TO PARLIAMENT

BY W. THWAITES,

TEN YEARS A HEAD SCHOOLMASTER IN EIGHT CONVICT ESTABLISHMENTS.

PRICE ONE SHILLING.

LONDON:

JUDD AND GLASS, NEW BRIDGE STREET, E. C.,

AND ALL BOOKSELLERS; MAY BE HAD ALSO OF THE AUTHOR.

MDCCCLXI.

OUR CONVICTS.

Whittington, near Stoke Ferry, Norfolk, 1861.

MY LORDS AND GENTLEMEN OF THE COMMONS OF ENGLAND,

The following pages are written to give you true information concerning the state and management of the Convicts in England, and to show through you to the country, why it is the prison at Chatham and the other convict prisons are so often disturbed by furious and murderous outbreaks on the part of the convicts imprisoned within them. This is the more necessary, as the Home Secretary, whose duty it is to be well-informed of the state of the convict prisons, has, as will be seen from the following quotation, expressed himself quite unable to give any information as to the causes of the late bloody riots in Chatham prison:—

THE CONVICT REVOLT AT CHATHAM.

Mr. Alderman SALOMONS asked the Secretary of State for the Home Department if he could give any information concerning the outbreaks of the convicts at Chatham; if he was aware of any alleged causes for those outrages; and what steps had been taken to prevent their recurrence?

" Sir G. C. LEWIS believed the most satisfactory way of answering the question of his hon. friend, would be to state shortly what had taken place with reference to the recent disturbance in the prison at Chatham. Early in January, six of the prisoners attempted to escape. The attempt was frustrated, and they were removed to the Penitentiary at Millbank. Early in the present month, a disturbance occurred while the convicts employed in a small island in the Medway, called St. Mary's Island, were at dinner. The ground alleged by the convicts implicated in that disturbance was the poverty of the soup furnished to them for their dinner. That complaint, however, was entirely unfounded. It was merely a pretext for a disturbance. These men were removed to separate cells to await the decision of the Director of Prisons. Captain Gambier went down last Monday to try them, when it was reported to him that the other men-convicts were in a state of insubordination. A number of the men then began shouting and

B

throwing up their hats. They were separated from the others by the civil guard, and the remainder were ordered by the governor to return to prison. Some of the convicts obeyed the order, and were locked up in their respective cells. Others then began shouting and making disturbances. They shut the doors of the cells of the other prisoners, thereby preventing them from re-entering their cells. By this unruly conduct, the disturbance became general, and the excitement great. The governor of the prison and Captain Gambier remonstrated with them, and the military were sent for. During the interval that occurred before the arrival of the military, the convicts broke some of the windows, and upset some stores. That was almost the extent of the mischief which they did. As soon as the military arrived, order was restored without loss of life, and all the prisoners were locked up. It was not true that one of the warders had been severely injured, as stated in some of the newspapers. On the following day, Captain Gambier went down to the prison; forty-six of the ringleaders were convicted and sentenced to thirty-six lashes each. All the prisoners who had taken part in the disturbance were placed upon bread and water and confined to their cells. The hon. gentleman had asked him as to the cause of the serious disturbance amongst the convicts. He had investigated the matter with some care, and *regretted to say he was not, nor were the officers in the prison able to give a very satisfactory account of the precise cause* which produced this outbreak. But he understood the general cause of the disturbances at the prison was the importation into it of the refuse convicts at the hulks, where it was impossible to enforce strict discipline. There had been no change of discipline or diet to account for the outbreak, nor had any specific grievance been alleged, either before or after the outbreak, by any convict engaged in it.

My Lords and Gentlemen, if the outbreak at Chatham was an exceptional circumstance, it might be impossible to arrive at the cause, although it is not at all probable that 800 men out of 1,100 would be in open and furious mutiny without some tangible reason being alleged. Rebellion is the chronic condition of all the convict prisons. I spent ten years under Sir Joshua Jebb, as first schoolmaster among convicts; I served in eight different convict prisons and hulks, and in every one of them, from time to time, occurred furious and general revolts. On one occasion the assistant-surgeon, Charles Hope, Esq., was murdered. I left the convict service in 1857, and since that time the rebellions among the convicts have been more frequent, and of a far more fearful and general character. In Dartmoor, at Portsmouth, at Portland, at Lewes, and at Chatham, during the last three years there have been far more mutinies among the convicts than ever were known before.

It has been kept from the knowledge of the Lords and Commons, but those acquainted with convicts well know that mutiny and riot are far more general in Sir J. Jebb's convict prisons than they ever were even in the horrible hulks.

Sir J. Jebb, for a series of years, was in the habit, as his reports to Parliament will show, of casting all the blame attaching to his management upon the pernicious effect of the hulks. The hulks have been abolished now four years : the convicts trained in them have been set at liberty ; and the convicts now in the different prisons are the very cream of Sir J. Jebb's prison management. Consequently the results are all the more striking. Under the hulk system the convicts were kept in some control, with fewer appliances, and at much less expense—horrible though that system was. Under Sir J. Jebb's system we have palatial prisons, expensive management, and enormous expense, and the convicts wax in discipline and morals worse and worse. Hence the system of Sir J. Jebb has strikingly broke down, and has manifested itself—so far as the discipline and management of the convicts go—very far inferior to the much decried (and by no one more than by Sir Joshua) hulk system.

Sir J. Jebb has gained knighthood upon the strength, not of success, but of the failure of his attempt to manage properly the convicts of England. He has been allowed to write flattering blue books upon his own system ; has been permitted to print and circulate them at public expense. Those blue books have for years studiously withheld from Parliament what ought to have been known, while they have unduly puffed a system which in its details contains many of the worst features of the tyranny and corruption of the prisons of Naples.

Successive Home Secretaries, and none more than Sir G. Grey, have, against the interests of the country, handed over the convict service to the irresponsible control of Sir J. Jebb, until that service has become, as these pages will prove, a disgrace to the justice, the morality, and the Christianity of England.

It is not my intention, in these pages, to burden your Lordships and Gentlemen with a mass of details ; my object is to urge upon you the great need of a *searching public inquiry into the effects of Sir J. Jebb's convict system, and the fearful abuses his management has fostered ; likewise, how demoralising upon both officers and convicts*— details I reserve to bring before any *public inquiry* that the Parliament or Government may institute. The present object is to give a bird's-eye view of the state and management of the convicts, and the immoral influences brought to bear upon them, under the name of a humane and reformatory discipline. When I have related a few facts, and published a few documents, you will then see what a mass of evidence is forthcoming to prove that Sir J. Jebb has been allowed to deceive the country while reaping honours and fame to himself.

The first fact I will adduce is, that riotous conduct is the chronic condition of the convicts in Sir Joshua's prisons, and that by rebellion the convicts have invariably obtained under him, a redress of their real and their assumed grievances.

In 1848, there was a great riot of convicts at Woolwich, under the governor, Mr. L. T———. After the riot, the convicts obtained redress; and Mr. L. T——— was ordered to discontinue the treatment that had driven the convicts as a body to revolt.

In 1849, there was a great revolt of convicts at Portsmouth under both Major S—— and Captain B——.

At Woolwich in the same year there were repeated revolts, and redress was given the convicts.

In the years 1850 and 1851 there were repeated revolts of the convicts at Shorncliffe, at Dartmoor, and outbreaks at Portland; again the convicts got redress.

In the years 1852, 1853, 1854, and 1855 there were several outbreaks in the different prisons; but the most remarkable and the most lamentable in its results was the outbreak at Gosport, when the convicts *complained of the food, of the tyranny of the officers, and of the neglect of the Convict Board of Directors.* At that time, Surgeon Charles Hope was cruelly murdered; his murder is a lasting disgrace upon the Directors of Prisons, as he was made by the convicts a sacrifice to draw upon that prison the attention of the authorities. Immediately after that foul murder, the convicts obtained from Sir J. Jebb all they clamoured for; thus at least offering to convicts a premium for revolt and murder. I shall have again to refer to this particular in another part.

In the year 1857, the convicts at Woolwich set fire to their prison ship, the *Defence,* and destroyed that vessel. During the same year, the same body of convicts at Lewes broke into fearful revolt, broke all their windows, assaulted the surgeon, and threatened to murder the governor and deputy. The Rev. G. Cookesley was at the prison at the time, and he and the schoolmasters were the only superior officers that dared go among the convicts. After that riot, the convicts again obtained redress at the hands of the Directors, and a stop was put to the arbitrary conduct of the officers, especially of the Governor, Captain W——, who had illegally taken away a portion of their food, and acted most harshly towards them.

In 1858, 1859, 1860, and now in 1861, there have been more alarming riots at Portsmouth, at Portland, and Chatham; while in former days fifty or a hundred convicts revolted, now we have fierce rebellion of hundreds of furious and enraged men. I will not here insert anything of my own, but am content to let the public papers speak upon the matter. The first quotation is from the *Globe* of September 28th, 1858 :—

CONVICT REVOLT AT PORTLAND.

At last we have something like a descriptive report of the outbreak among the prisoners at Portland Island, on the 13th instant. The event is *remarkable in many ways,* and we are not disposed to *prejudge* it; but the notice attracted by such facts as are known will *stimulate inquiry* to give us the amplest materials for judgment. The provoking cause of outbreak is well understood. In 1853 an Act was passed regulating sentence of penal servitude as distinct from the sentences of transportation. Convicts who were well-behaved were allowed a partial remission of their sentence ; but under the Act of 1853, in certain cases, imprisonment at home was regarded as a commutation of the sentence of transportation, and in these cases the period of home servitude was carried out to the full extent. The Act passed in 1857 abolished the distinction between transportation and penal servitude, leaving the good behaviour of the convict to earn for him the remission of some part of his sentence. The effect in the prison is, that men confined under sentences previous to 1853, and those under the existing Act, may, on good behaviour, enjoy a certain remission of the sentence ; whereas prisoners sentenced between '53 and '57 are apparently doomed to go through their full term. It seems that this distinction has created a bad feeling ; although in a *semi-official* statement at the end of last week it was reported that the convicts at the Portland Prison had, " ever since its formation in 1848, and up to this point, been conspicuous for their good feeling and industry." The reader will have observed the essential difference between the kinds of sentence and the simply *apparent* nature of the injustice endured by the convict sentenced between '53 and '57 ; but on the surface, in a rough and ready practical way, such as is likely to present itself to the mind of a rude, impatient, uninformed man, there is a distinction which might engender invidious feeling. In passing, however, we cannot avoid noticing one circumstance, which *qualifies this view.* The outbreak of the 13th *does not appear to have been limited to any particular section of prisoners*, classed by sentences, but to have originated in a section classified with reference entirely to other considerations. It is the quarriers of Verne Hill that appear to have taken part in the conspiracy—a class which we have before had occasion to notice.

Another circumstance comes out in the descriptive report upon the tumultuary attempt ; it is, that the conspiracy had been going on at least for some days ; so much so that a casual visitor to Weymouth, whose report we have, and who tells us that he " had no connection with the prison," heard of the conspiracy on the previous Saturday— the 11th. He purchased a revolver, and took up his station as a spectator to witness the performance. *The Government had been equally informed*, and stood prepared for the whole proceeding. The affair commenced about a quarter to seven o'clock on Monday morning, when the convicts streamed from the prison gates under a guard, and poured forth to take their places in the quarry behind the prison. There they stood, " about a *thousand* of the most formidable ruffians" whom an " Eye-Witness" ever saw. Perhaps the aspect of the men might be somewhat modified in the sight of the " Eye-Witness" by the peculiar character in which they then appeared on that stage. They had, however, been selected, as we have said, not on the score of their sentence and its chronology, but on the strength of their muscular power and their fitness for quarry work. They stood for a time idling under the bright sun, apparently hesitating to commence their work, really awaiting a preconcerted signal. Suddenly, a shout was raised ; 30 or 40 men jumped upon one of the raised tramways which divide the quarry, and attempted to rush beyond the official bounds; intending to overpower the guards, burn the prison, plunder the villages, escape to the mainland, and become lost in the general body of "the dangerous classes." But the Government stood prepared; 200 civil guards and warders, and 150 Wexford militia, were on the spot; and the convicts no sooner made their sudden outbreak, than small piquets of the Wexfords appeared on the elevated tramway, and at other points, like the sudden appearance of the clans in the scene of the "Donna del Lago." The herd of convicts was under the control of bayonets and a cross fire. The active rioters gave way, suffered themselves to be driven into small buildings, and were put in chains. During the day there were "spasmodic rushes of the men, who were kept in check by the swords of the warders," and the renewed presence of the Wexfords. On Tuesday, the men probably thinking that the officials regarded the conspiracy as over, and presuming the military to be withdrawn, there was a new outbreak, with a repetition of the same scene as on the Monday. On the Wednesday the men remained sulky; and even on the Thursday an experienced *warder* judged from their "*phizzyhogs*" that some of them were wavering—particularly one man, who laboured under the damnatory attributes of Irish birth and "grey eyes." But the warder gave that man good advice, and "tried to point out the folly of his projects." Of course the conspiracy was put down, and the order of the United Kingdom will not be disturbed by the machinations of convict mutineers in Portland Prison.

The event came *as a most dramatic commentary* on a controversy which we had noticed a very short time before; we allude to the published comments and replications of Colonel Jebb and Captain Walter Crofton on the English and Irish systems of convict prisons—systems which stand perfectly independent in their administrations, and are based on principles materially 'different. The Irish system proceeds upon a principle of actively calling forth the industry of the convict, while supplying him with a practical training and with information in a form suited to enlighten his mind, and not *spontaneously administered by jailors who talk about "phizzyhogs ;"* and after a rather severe chastising discipline in prison, it accustoms him to a gradual exercise of freedom. In the course of this controversy, Colonel Jebb endeavoured to show that there is less difference between the English and Irish systems than the Irish officials represented. He expressed a conviction that in the Portland system "the Government had gone quite as far in the way of encouragement, relaxation, and discipline, and care for the prisoner's best interests during confinement, as is either expedient or necessary." He reported that "*new hopes, new resolutions, and better feelings had been imparted* to the prisoners." But he spoke indifferently of a common room as not having conduced to moral feeling; and he described Verne Hill as presenting the parallel of that system of working in rural districts, the convicts housed in iron huts, which has been adopted in Ireland. *In the midst of this controversy the convicts themselves suddenly come forward to take part in it.* Amongst the differences between the English and Irish systems, is a very much higher rate of dietary in the Portland Prison; and one of the serjeants in the Wexford Militia, "an old Ghuznee stormer," confided to the "Eye-

Witness" his opinion " it was not right for the prisoners to have *p'huddn* (pudding) three times a week, and a soldier none." The Irish dietary is much more stern. It is a circumstance which *piques curiosity*, that this *conspiracy* was *suffered* to develope itself until it became the overt act with which the *whole thousand displayed undisguised sympathy*, instead of being nipped in the bud by withdrawing the ringleaders. We have, however, no sufficient information to arrive at any conclusion on the subject. It simply *challenges notice* for some of the *remarkable phenomena* to which we have referred ; and it will unquestionably excite an increased interest in those who are watching the two systems, English and Irish, in order to compare their practical results.—*Globe*, Thursday, Sept. 23.

EFFECTS OF MILBANK TRAINING.

About eight o'clock on Tuesday morning a confusion and alarm never witnessed before took place on the South-Western Railway, Waterloo-road, London, a gang of no less than eighty convicts refusing to proceed by the regular train to Portland. The persuasions of the officers were useless, and it was ultimately deemed expedient to send to Millbank Prison for the governor and additional guard, when, after two hours' delay, the convicts were forwarded on their journey.—From the *North Kent Advertiser* of November 27, 1858.

It would swell these pages too inordinately to quote from the *Times* its account of riots at Dartmoor and Portland. I shall therefore upon this topic content myself with a quotation the most truthful to be found (though quite incorrect as to the cause of the outbreak), of the latest proof of the excellency of Sir. J. Jebb's Convict System ; it is from the *Chatham News* of Feb. 14th, 1861. And as I have been assured by one who knows the exact condition of Chatham Prison, it is far short of the case,—and quite wrong in its guesses of the causes of the outbreak.

CONVICT MUTINIES AT CHATHAM.

The mutinous spirit manifested by the convicts at St. Mary's Prison for some time past, unquelled by the punishments inflicted on the ring-leaders, broke forth at the end of last week and the beginning of this with redoubled violence, so that on Monday it was feared that nothing less than a sacrifice of life by the warders and military firing on the rebellious felons collected in the prison would crush the mutiny and restore order. Thus in the afternoon it was reported and believed in the towns that no fewer than five lives had been sacrificed—those of two warders and three prisoners : happily this turned out to be an exaggeration ; but the reality was bad enough. It has been exceedingly difficult to obtain authentic particulars of the successive mutinies ; but we subjoin as accurate an account of the facts as we can collect, warning the reader that there may be errors in it. The reckless nature of the prisoners is very apparent from one consideration—they all knew that almost within call there was an overpowering military force, which, if need were, would assuredly quell a convict rebellion by shooting down the rebels—even this did not deter the ruffians. No doubt Government will institute a searching investigation into the causes of these outbreaks ; though it is easy to guess that if two or three daring villains once commence a resistance to authority in a case like this, the evil example will spread like wildfire among the dreadful crowd around them, ever prone to mischief and violence.

The utmost horror and alarm has been accasioned among the officials and others connected with the convict prison at Chatham, in consequence of a series of mutinous outbreaks by a portion of the convicts, amounting to several hundred of the most desperate characters, the behaviour and conduct of the prisoners concerned in the outbreaks being of a far more violent character than that which occurred at the mutiny a few weeks since. On the present occasion the convicts concerned in the first outbreak were all employed outside the prison on the occasion of the disturbance, and this, of course, rendered the situation of affairs the more alarming. In order to give a succinct narrative of the occurrence, it should be stated that of the thousand convicts belonging to the establishment at Chatham, several hundreds are daily employed in Chatham Dockyard, and a party of several hundred working on St. Mary's Island, adjoining the dockyard, whilst the remainder are employed in various ways on the roads and other Government works in the garrison. The party engaged in the first outbreak were those at work on St. Mary's Island, on which the whole of the occurrences took place.

At the usual hour on Friday morning about 400 of the convicts were marched down to the island to commence work, about thirty warders, all well armed, being in charge of them. Most of the men employed on the island are purposely sent there to work on account of their bad character, in order to remove them from any associates they might form in the dockyard or elsewhere, St. Mary's Island being altogether secluded. The convicts proceeded with their work all the morning until the hour for dinner. It is customary for about 300 of the men always to dine on the island, in a large building provided for that purpose, the remainder returning to the prison. The dinners of those who remain on the island are always sent to them, each convict being allowed for his dinner one pint of soup, a pound of potatoes, a certain quantity of meat, and six ounces of bread—a meal which is stated to be far better than that supplied to the unfortunate paupers in many of the workhouses. On Friday the convicts were in charge of a chief warder, named Burton, and on the soup being served out to the prisoners, many of them declared that it was "not good enough " for them, one of them dashing the contents of his basin into the face of Mr. Burton. This was the signal for a general uproar, and the contents of innumerable basins were thrown over the chief warder, who was drenched to the skin. The warders who were locked inside with the convicts in vain endeavoured to restore order, but the ringleaders threatened to murder them if they attempted to interfere, and then commenced smashing the windows and throwing their cups and tins about. They also commenced tearing up the tables and stools and armed themselves with the fragments, at the same time hooting and yelling in the most horrible manner. One of the convicts, who goes by the name of "Bassett," mounted a table and harangued his fellow-prisoners in violent terms, exhorting them to free themselves and not to return to their work. He also entreated them to stand by each other, and to kill any of the warders who attempted to interfere. This was followed by loud shouts, after which Bassett called for a song, and the whole number shouted out several low songs in chorus. During the uproar the warders in charge of the men used every endeavour, by entreaty and otherwise, to bring them to a state of subordination; but without effect, and the comparatively small number of warders in the island left them quite at the mercy of the convicts.

It is usual for the convicts to be locked in during the dinner hour, and immediately the outbreak commenced they demanded to be released. This, however, was not complied with, but immediately the dinner hour had expired the doors were unlocked, with the hope that the men would resume their work. Directly the convicts were released a few of them went towards their work with the intention of resuming it, but the others, released from all comparative control, smashed the windows of the adjoining building, tore down the spouts from the roof, and endeavoured to wrench off the bars from the windows, but these defied their strength. A number of free workmen on the island were so alarmed that they rushed to their boats and rowed off into the middle of the river. Several gentlemen on the opposite side of the harbour, hearing the uproar, and making out the mutinous state the convicts were in, put off for the island, but the most fearful threats were used towards them, which rendered it unsafe for them to attempt to land. The convicts all this while were destroying everything they could find on the island, the regulation boards being broken up and thrown into the river, their tin cups and cans being also thrown away, and several of them, taking off their serge coats and filling them with stones, hurled them also into the river.

In order to obtain the assistance of the warders at the prison, and also that of the military, the alarm-signal was hoisted, but its purport did not appear to be understood, as no assistance arrived from the prison or garrison for some time, when one of the principal warders arrived in a boat. The convicts, however, threatened him that he should be murdered if he landed, but the warder succeeded in getting ashore on a secluded part of the island. By this time numbers of the convicts had resumed their work, several of the more desperate characters, however, still continued their excesses.

It might seem a matter of surprise that none of the warders attempted to fire on any of the convicts. The prison regulations, however, positively forbid firing on any convict unless he attempts to escape or assault a warder, in which latter case he may be run through with the bayonet. Although during the outbreak the most fearful threats were used towards the warders, yet not one of them was struck, which accounts for no severe measures being taken. Towards five o'clock, the hour for leaving work, most of the mutineers had calmed down, and the opportunity was then taken to remove nearly the whole to the prison. Several of the ringleaders were left on the island, and an extra number of warders having then arrived, these were secured and all chained together, and removed to one cell, to await punishment.

A full report of the circumstances was made by the governor to the Home Secretary, and an investigation was ordered to be instituted by Captain Gambier, the Director-General. During Saturday and Sunday the men confined kept up a continual disturbance in their cells by hooting, kicking and yelling. The whole of the warders were on duty on Sunday, in case of a fresh outbreak.

The insubordination which prevailed last week continued until Monday, when the culminating point in the disturbances appeared to be attained, a scene of riot occurring within the prison which is described by the prison officials as being of the most appalling character.

Immediately after the outbreak on Friday, about twenty of the principal actors in that mutiny were chained together and placed in one cell, to await an order from Captain Gambier as to the punishment to be inflicted on them. Throughout the whole of Saturday and following days these men kept up a continual disturbance in the prison, which was taken up by the other convicts in the cells, and at times the noises made by their hootings and yells were completely overpowering. Captain Gambier, the Inspector-General of Convict Prisons, arrived at the establishment on Monday for the purpose of inquiring into the recent mutinous outbreak, and his presence at the prison soon became known among the inmates. During the morning the men were marched to their labours as usual in the dockyard, on St. Mary's Island, and at the other public works, although from the manner of most of them it was apparent to the officials that there was an undercurrent of mischief at work. The convicts returned to the prison at the customary hour for their dinner, which was served to them as usual, when several again complained of the badness of the food, although, as above remarked, the prison diet is greatly superior to that given in any union workhouse. The convicts, however, finished their dinner without making any disturbance, but on being ordered to resume their work numbers of them declared that they would not, and dared the keepers to interfere to make them. At this time it became known that several of the convicts concerned in the recent outrage had been ordered by Captain Gambier to be flogged, and afterwards sent back to Millbank and Pentonville, and this circumstance is believed to have greatly exasperated the convicts. On the usual gangs being formed in the prison yard, several of the convicts again refused to go to their work, and some of them commenced assaulting the keepers and warders who had them in their charge. At a preconcerted signal about fifty convicts made a sudden rush on the keepers, whom they quickly succeeded in overpowering, and almost at the same instant the other convicts, who were out of their cells waiting to commence work, turned upon their keepers, assailing them with fearful oaths, and threatened to massacre the whole of them. At this time several hundred convicts were free from all control, and the keys of the cells having been forced from the warders, those who were in the cells were quickly released.

The wildest uproar now ensued, the whole of the prisoners being loose within the prison, and ready for any excesses. Captain Gambier, who happened to be within the building, together with Captain Powell, the governor, Mr. Measor, deputy-governor, and the other principal officers of the establishment, were soon among the convicts, whom they endeavoured to induce to proceed to their cells. Having, however, to contend with upwards of 1,000 of the most depraved ruffians, and the guard only numbering 150 men, their efforts were entirely useless, and, from the fierce threats used towards the officers, there is little doubt that murder would have been committed had any attempt to interfere with the convicts been resorted to. After overpowering the keepers, a large body of convicts rushed to the office of the chief clerk, where they commenced destroying all the books, papers, accounts, and other official documents connected with the prison, smashing the whole of the windows, and destroying every article of furniture on which they could wreak their vengeance. An attempt was then made to set fire to the prison, and the building was actually fired in several places. The warders, however, at great risk to themselves, got out the hose and also the fire engine, which is always kept ready at the prison, and succeeded in extinguishing the flames. Numerous bands of convicts then proceeded to destroy every article within the prison on which they could lay their hands, valuable clocks being wantonly smashed, and several costly instruments called "noctaries," which are used at night to register the visits of the warders, being smashed to atoms. Scarcely a pain of glass was left whole in the prison, the most terrible havoc being committed on everything which came in the way of the infuriated ruffians. The large stove placed in the centre of the building for the purpose of warming the prison was turned bodily over, and much injured. The amount of damage committed is estimated at £1,000.

An eye-witness of the scene of destruction presented by the interior of the prison—at least those parts to which the convicts had access—describes it to us as " wonderful,"—it was marvellous how the prisoners, of course at the outset without weapons, managed to break iron window-frames, iron bars, &c., and create such a scene of ruin as the military beheld when they entered the prison.

As soon as it was ascertained that all hope of restoring order, without the assistance of the military, was at an end, messengers were despatched to the garrison for a strong body of troops, and also to the dockyard for the Metropolitan police and the guard always on duty at that establishment. Immediately on receiving the order, a strong body of police, under the direction of Inspector Pethers, quickly proceeded to the prison. A party of the Royal Marines, who happened to be engaged in rifle firing near the prison, also proceeded to the convict establishment, under the command of Major Rodney. On receipt of the order for the military at the garrison, a body of 400 of the Royal Marines, the 4th and 35th Companies of the Royal Engineers, together with upwards of 500 troops of the line, were quickly despatched to the prison; Colonel Jervis, Colonel Harness, C.B., and the other principal officers of the garrison, also proceeding there to direct the operations of the soldiers. Each of the troops had with him ten rounds of ball cartridge. On the arrival of the military at the prison, a considerable time was permitted to elapse before they were allowed to enter, the reason for which could not be understood, especially as it was evident from the noise and uproar, which could be distinctly heard outside, that the mutineers were in full possession of the prison—probably a motive of humanity kept back military force as long as possible. After some time the military were allowed to enter, when several hundred men were ordered to charge the rioters within the prison, about 300 of the troops being judiciously posted outside to prevent any of the convicts escaping. The moment the convicts caught sight of the soldiery, they set up the most fearful yells, and challenged them with oaths to "Come on." The order was then given to charge the convicts, the keepers driving the prisoners before them with their truncheons, which they used with great effect. The troops continued to drive the prisoners before them, but no attempt was made to fire on them, although the soldiers repeatedly requested their officers to be allowed to do so. In a very short time after the arrival of the military, the whole of the convicts had been driven into their cells, where they were securely fastened. A portion of the troops were then sent back to their barracks, but several hundred men of the Royal Marines, the Engineers, and the Line remained on duty at the prison all night, and also on the following day, in case there should be any attempt at another outbreak.

About forty of the ringleaders in the revolt were seized in the afternoon, and, each having been heavily iron, the whole were chained together, and placed in one cell, with a strong guard over them. On Tuesday morning, Captain Gambier having ascertained the names of the principal parties concerned in the outrage and mutiny, directed that forty of them should each receive three dozen lashes. An order was at once despatched to the Marine Barracks for the halberds and cats, which were immediately sent to the prison, eight of the strongest drummers being at the same time despatched to administer the punishment, which was inflicted in the presence of a strong body of troops.

The whole of the convicts were kept confined in their cells on Tuesday, and no repetition of the disturbances was attempted, a strong body of troops being still at the prison.

During the height of the disturbances on Monday, one of the convict-keepers, named Goad, was severely injured by the convicts, and was considered to be in a very precarious state. On the outbreak occurring the convicts demanded that Mr. Kinch, the chief warder, and Goad should be given up to them, as they intended to hang them. Goad, had he been recognised, would no doubt have fallen a victim to their fury, but after being severely treated he was forced into a cell, where he was locked in.

On Tuesday morning, Major-General Sir Joshua Jebb, K.C.B., the Inspector-General of Prisons, arrived at the prison to institute an investigation into the outbreak, in conjunction with Captain Gambier. The result of their investigation was made known in the evening—ninety of the ringleaders being ordered to be flogged, and afterwards sent to Millbank and Pentonville. Twelve men were flogged at the prison on Tuesday afternoon, including Bassett, who was the ringleader in the outrage on St. Mary's Island, a notorious convict named Butt, and ten others, each of whom received three dozen lashes.

The ringleaders in the mutiny were securely chained together, awaiting their punishment. A guard of 100 soldiers, with loaded rifles, remained on duty at the prison on Tuesday night.

One account which has appeared states that "the lower part of the prison presented the appearance of a slaughter-house, blood flowing in streams in all directions. Tables, chairs, gas-pipes, and windows were broken; and, indeed, everything that the convicts could lay their hands on. The ruffians armed themselves with the legs of the tables and pieces of the iron bars to defend themselves against the soldiers. In one portion of the building they had collected a large quantity of the broken wood and books and papers, which they set fire to. Fortunately it was extinguished before any serious damage had been done. All the chairs and desks in the offices were broken, and a large portion of flooring was ripped up, and the books kept relating to the whole of the establishment were torn to pieces and thrown out through the broken windows. It appears that several of the convicts, when they were disarmed by the military, were found to have in their possession copies of several of the London weekly newspapers. How they obtained them no one can tell, as newspapers are prohibited in the prison.

Among the reports that have been circulated, was one that Mr. Frazier, a warder, died on Tuesday from ill-treatment by the convicts. It is, unfortunately, true that this warder died on Tuesday, but it was from disease of the lungs, from which he had suffered some time. During the late disturbances, he was an occupant of the infirmary, and was not at all engaged in quieting them. Mr. Frazier was a widower; and he has left four children.

As may readily be supposed, the tidings that a large body of soldiers had been called in to quell a mutiny at St. Mary's Prison rapidly spread through the Towns on Monday afternoon, and caused no small excitement, and gave rise to many conjectures and rumours. In the neighbourhood of the prison, the horrible hubbub created by a thousand felons in mutiny, and the arrival of bodies of troops, attracted much attention, and many persons congregated. The Dockyard walls, the piles of timber, &c., were covered by the artisans, attracted from their labours by the din.

Colonel Sir Joshua Jebb, Inspector-General of Military Prisons, who arrived on Tuesday at the convict prison, completed his investigation, and left the same evening for London, to lay the report before the Secretary of State for the Home Department. The inquiry was made in conjunction with Captain Gambier, the Principal Director of Convict Establishments, and the Governor of the Prison, Captain Powell. They were occupied nearly the whole of the day in examining the keepers, warders, and all other persons connected with the establishment, and the inquiry led to ten of the most violent of the ringleaders being flogged, and on Wednesday morning there were thirty more similarly punished. These ruffians only received three dozen each, the punishment being inflicted by able-bodied drummers from the Royal Marines and regiments of the line, and some of the sailors from her Majesty's ship Wellesley, 72. The men flogged were those who took a leading part in the revolt on Monday afternoon. The drummers engaged in flogging the convicts were occupied at the task the whole of the morning, and also part of the afternoon, the convicts being punished one at a time. Each man, after receiving his punishment, was conveyed to the prison infirmary, to be medically treated. It was remarked that the convicts who behaved in the most outrageous manner during the outbreak were those whose cries were the loudest during the infliction of the punishment, each lash being administered with telling effect by the drummers engaged in the task, which duty they appeared to perform with anything but regret, so detested is the conduct of the convicts by them. Many of the prisoners bore their punishment uttering scarcely a single cry. Several of the men on being released from the triangles behaved with the greatest bravado, notwithstanding the intense pain they were enduring, and frequent threats were made that the "business was not yet done," and that on the first opportunity murder would be committed.

Mr. Goad, one of the warders, who received severe injuries about the head, for a time was in a precarious state. The alleged causes of this revolt are bad provisions and short supply of their daily rations. How far this is well grounded may be judged from the fact that they have one pint of cocoa, with bread and butter, for breakfast; six ounces of cooked meat, without bone or gristle, and one pound of vegetables, for dinner; and for tea they have a pint of gruel or tea, whichever they choose. It is a fact that the convicts live better than the honest working labourer; their bread is the best that can be obtained, and the meat which is supplied to the prison is said to be much better than what is served out to the troops in the garrison.

The convicts were kept confined to their cells the whole day on Wednesday, and none left the prison to work. The troops remained on guard at the prison until further orders from Major-General Eyre. Each of the drummers employed in flogging the convicts will be paid extra for that not very pleasant duty.

Later in the week, numbers more of the worst offenders were flogged. Order had been so far restored on Thursday, that a portion of the convicts resumed their ordinary labours in the Dockyard. The warder Goad is much better. He has but recently joined the prison from Dartmoor, and was recognised by old occupants of that gaol, who had been punished there through his instrumentality; they struck and kicked him so violently that he was carried to the hospital in a state of insensibility.

THE DEPUTY-GOVERNOR'S STATEMENT.

Mr. C. P. Measor has corrected some errors which have got into the papers.

"It was not the governor's office, but the chief warder's, which is in the interior of the prison, which the convicts sacked. It is within too easy access of their cells, and they wreaked their vengeance accordingly upon the papers and reports of that indefatigable officer, instead, as some of the most brutal would have rejoiced to do, upon his person.

"No unnecessary time was allowed to elapse between the arrival of the troops, and the measures which they so successfully adopted to take possession of the interior of the building, and drive the prisoners to their cells. It was, however, quite necessary that the commanding officers should first be informed of the locality, and given a sight of the ground plan of the building, which was immediately done; but I have no doubt that the soldiers, between whom and the convicts there is no love lost, considering their being on as good a scale of living, were not a little impatient to get at them. To avoid disastrous consequences, and the unnecessary effusion of blood, it was desirable that only really effective measures should be adopted, and this was the sole wish both of the Director and Governor, while as soon as the troops could be advantageously posted an entrance was effected.

" The causes assigned by the convicts for their outbreak are the severity of some of the officers and the quality of their diet. Neither has the least foundation in fact. Every complaint of the prisoners against their officers has ever received full consideration at the hands of the Governor, and, instead of any tyranny being practised, it may be doubted whether undue leniency has not occasionally been shown them by some of the warders; and, as to the quality of their diet, I can answer for it, from daily inspection, that it has been undeniable. Men in the position of criminals, who get 27 oz. of excellent white bread, 5 or 6 oz. of good beef, three quarters of a pint of by no means indifferent soup, and cocoa and gruel in addition, as their ordinary diet, cannot be said either to have much grievance on the ground of quantity."

Enough has been said to show that Sir J. Jebb's system is anything but one that promotes order and discipline among convicts. Let me now bring before you four letters which I had the honour to write for the *Daily News* and *Times* in the summer of 1856, in which I proved that Sir J. Jebb's prisons are not what he styles them, Reformatories.

I need not here again attempt to prove this, as there can be no reformation in an atmosphere of perpetual revolt. I shall allow my letters to speak for themselves, just remarking, that if the subject was worthy of the press in that year, how much more now ?

TREATMENT OF CRIMINALS.

To the Editor of the " Times."

Sir,—You throw open your columns to prison directors, to visiting magistrates, members of Parliament, and voluntary philanthropists, to say their say upon the now all-important subject of criminal management.   Will you permit one who has spent the best portion of his life in the closest intimacy with criminals to offer a few remarks upon the treatment of our criminal classes ?   Sir, I often smile when I read the crude remarks which appear from time to time in the public press.   A gentleman visits a prison or a convict station ; he beholds everything neat and clean; outwardly all appears orderly and fair, and he goes away with the impression that what he has seen has proved that the criminals are under the best possible treatment for the eradication of their vice and the reformation of their morals.   But, Sir, too many of our prisons are only like the whited sepulchres of old—fair to the eye, but within full of every abomination.

Doubtless a report of a prison can be made to read well; it is easy to point to the order of the inmates, and to show that so many sermons

C

have been preached within the walls of the prison during the year; that each prisoner has had so many hours' instruction from duly-qualified schoolmasters; and that the prison books show a great diminution in the number of prison offences. All this, and more than this, may be reported of a prison, while at the same time that prison may be a festering mass of moral pollution. I see that your correspondent, Lord Robert Grosvenor, says that but few come out of prison contaminated. His experience and mine totally differ; few come out of any prison, that I am acquainted with, without adding some worse features to their moral character. I grant that if you keep a prisoner totally secluded, and never allow him to speak to another prisoner, he may not increase his vice, but such a man, if kept long in prison, will lose either health or intellect.

What is the fact with regard to the convict prisons? In those prisons the convicts have daily intercourse with each other; they converse at their work, as they work in gangs of from six to thirty men in one gang; there may be a regular burglar, a pickpocket, a fence or receiver of stolen goods, a young man who has committed his first breach of trust, a countryman for a breach of the game laws,—in fact, a gang of convicts at work is composed of criminals of every hue and dye. Now, Sir, what forms the staple of the conversation of these men while at work, or while exercising in their yards? It is, Sir, a recital of their past misdeeds, and very often they are engaged in laying plans for their future proceedings. Now, I would ask any candid mind if a moderate criminal can pass from two to four years in such an atmosphere without contamination? And let it be borne in mind that every one of our convict prisons offers at present this facility for the increase of vice.

There is no classification of criminals in convict prisons. The more hardened are mixed indiscriminately with the first offenders. Old and young labour together for weeks, months, and years; and, Sir, I can answer for it, as a most certain fact, that many a young man has left a convict prison determined to lead a life of crime who received his education to fit him for so doing from his comrades with whom he laboured and associated in a convict prison. Robberies have been planned by convicts while they were convicts—men who before they entered a convict prison were strangers to each other have gone forth sworn companions to prey upon the inhabitants of this land.

Your correspondent, Lord Robert Grosvenor, appears to think that the adult criminal should not receive so much attention as the neglected youth of the land. Now, Sir, I am alive to the fact that a neglected youthful population is a most fruitful source whence our criminal population springs; and that it is upon that class we must turn a considerable portion of our attention; but we have not now to deal with a criminal population that is to be; we have to grapple with a population of criminals that already exists. When a mighty torrent is upon us we have to think how to stem its force, to subdue its might, and to avert the destruction which it threatens. We do not then think only of the source whence it sprung. Even so is it with our criminal population —the mighty torrent is upon us, the surging waves of crime are rolling through our land. We are therefore called upon to grapple at once with the fearful mass. Our statesmen are called upon, not only to turn their attention whence it sprung, but to afford protection to the country against the fearful evil that is already in our midst.

Sir, every adult criminal is a teacher of crime. The Rev. Mr. Kingsmill mentions one convict who confessed that he had trained some hundreds of youths to commit crime; and I am aware from personal knowledge that thousands of our adult criminals live upon the proceeds of the crimes of those who have been trained by themselves. The London police can tell how the ticket-of-leave men in London now exist—not by their own acts, but by the acts of those who work under their auspices. Is it not become of the utmost importance to the nation to ask what is to be done with our adult criminals now that transportation has almost ceased? We must grapple, and grapple sternly, with our adult criminals; we must soon find out the best method of dealing with them, both to deter and to reform. It is not enough to talk philosophically of the sources of crime and the best means of drying up its fountains, we have the fearful evil in our midst, and, as with the cholera, we must adopt measures to get rid of the nuisance at once, and busy ourselves with its sources when we have manfully and wisely grappled with the thing itself.

I am one, Sir, who, from experience, sees the stern necessity of adopting more strenuous measures to deter and to reform our criminals. Our convict prisons, as at present administered, do neither the one nor the other. Ask those who are acquainted with them, and they will tell you that convicts as a body do not mind the discipline of our convict prisons; that they return to them as a matter of course; and that the convicts after several years spent within them depart, the great majority of them, unreformed.

We have not yet found a prison system that is a deterrent to the criminal, and much less have we introduced a system that is reformatory. I believe that the attention of the community must be drawn to the subject before such a prison system will be discovered. Until the present time the matter has been almost in the hands of one man, or at the most of a clique. Experiment upon experiment has been tried, but practical men—men who have a real knowledge of the criminal mind, have not been consulted; and is it strange that so little good has been the result?

Who are so well able to suggest what should be the mode of treatment towards the criminal as those who have spent years of intimacy with them? And yet these are the men who are never consulted. Men of theory, not men of practice, have had the management of our criminals, and the result is, we have tens of thousands of adult criminals now in our midst, who, after years of prison treatment, are very Pariahs in our land.

But I have made this letter too long to attempt to point out what I feel ought to be done. Should you honour me with its insertion I may venture to write what my experience of criminals would suggest as proper in their treatment.

Sept. 26, 1856.   DELTA.

c 2

To the Editor of the " Times."

Sir,—I am pledged to place before you what I conceive ought to be done to produce the reformation of the great criminal class of this country. I shall endeavour to accomplish my purpose in two ways—viz., by pointing out what I conceive is defective in the mode now adopted, and also by suggestions which have forced themselves upon my mind through a long intercourse with the criminal classes.

I am compelled to state, first, that the present mode adopted with convicts is not deterrent. Those who are acquainted with convict establishments are cognizant of this fact, that regular criminals return again and again; and why is this? The reason is convict prisons have but few terrors to those who have graduated in them. There they mix up with their boon companions; they are warmly clothed, well fed, have every medical comfort, and can see their friends once every quarter; they can correspond very frequently; and they certainly are not overworked.

The discipline they are brought under is not very rigid; in fact, the criminal now finds that from first to last in a convict prison he has only to keep a civil tongue in his head, and he will get through his imprisonment easily enough. He also finds that the authorities are very careful to keep him, while a prisoner, in a good humour, and in order to do so, he is offered extra allowances of bread and cheese and beer, over and above the usual prison diet. In a word, quietness and falling in with the prison routine will enable a convict to get through his penal servitude with far less hardships than fall to the lot of tens of thousands of honest hard-working men.

I would suggest that penal servitude during its first stages should entail actual hardship upon those who deserve it; that a man's food should be hardly earned before he ate it; that he should be obliged to work himself out of this primary stage by the most exemplary conduct; that no soothing should be adopted to get him to conform to the prison rules, but that stern necessity should teach him that to better himself, and to get into the second stage, he must prove himself worthy of it.

I would at once abolish the indiscriminate association of criminals. There should be a classification according to their offences and antecedents. The more vicious should no longer have it in their power to corrupt, as at present, the less depraved. This could easily be avoided by taking care to place in each working party men whose casts of mind and mode of life had been the same. In their hours of work improper conversation should be really, not as now nominally, prevented.

Every prisoner who came into prison ignorant of reading and writing should not be allowed to make any progress towards any amelioration of his prison condition unless he showed an effort to improve his mind. A sound, practical education should be offered, and all who would not avail themselves of it should not be put forward for a mitigation of sentence. This education should not be afforded during the ordinary hours of work, but after the performance of their daily duties. Each prisoner ignorant of a trade should be allowed to learn one, after he had passed in an exemplary manner through his first course of penal drudgery.

No regular thief should be allowed to return to his old haunts with a ticket-of-leave, and no prisoner be allowed his conditional pardon without having first proved his fitness by mental and industrial improvement, and there having been secured for him *bona fide* employment. The system of patronage, I am certain, is needed, if we are to deal satisfactorily with our liberated convicts.

Longer periods of penal servitude are needed, the criminal being able to shorten them by his manifest improvement.

My experience with criminals has taught me that crime springs from what I may term a mental malady. It is therefore necessary to deal with the mind of criminals in all efforts that we make for their reformation. I am therefore more strongly convinced than ever that mere discipline, however good, and prisons, however well constructed, will never act beneficially in decreasing crime until mind is brought to bear upon the diseased mind of the criminal. Government has proved its appreciation of this in the erection and discipline of its model prisons, such as Pentonville and Wakefield, but has almost ignored it in the great prisons for convicts on public works. How often have I heard it said by criminals that they felt a hatred of their past life through the influences brought to bear upon them in such prisons as Pentonville, but they lost all good feeling as soon as they got to the associated work! Sir, evil communications do corrupt good manners, and if we are to improve our criminals we must take more care in their classification.

But criminal improvement depends mainly—may I not say almost entirely?—upon the persons to whom they are intrusted for management. A ship needs a navigator to take it safely through a dangerous sea; an army needs more than valour or animal " pluck," it needs a general to direct and command. Criminals need the most peculiar management; they should be intrusted to the care of those who are acquainted with their peculiar character, and who have given their minds to the subject.

I have perceived that Captain Maconnochie, in his evidence before the Transportation Committee, complains that prisons are too much in the hands of military men. Now, Sir, there can be no objection to military men if they are men who are acquainted with the subject,—men who by temper and morals, as well as by knowledge, are fitted to manage criminals. Colonel Jebb is a military man, and if his reports express his own views, and are an index of his own mind, he proves himself highly fitted for his work. But, Sir, he having been a colonel is no proof that he is the man to whom criminals should be intrusted. That fitness he has proved independent of his army rank. Army discipline is not the best for criminals. You may have a perfect piece of machinery in a prison, but you will leave the minds of the criminals untouched.

At present convicts are almost entirely intrusted to gentlemen from the army ; a civilian, however fitted he may be, has no hope, no chance, of being intrusted with the management of convicts unless he has influence. I would suggest that our convict prisons be thrown open to the country, that the convict service be no longer an adjunct to the army, but that civilians be as eligible as colonels, majors, and captains to fill the offices of governors and deputy-governors of our prisons.

In the convict service, as in every other, I would have the right man in the right place. A governor should not be the head of a perfect piece of routine, but should be selected because of his known fitness to act as a criminal reformer. He should be a man who had qualified himself for his office, and his appointment should be an encouragement to all who worked under him; so that the humblest officer might perceive that fitness and merit were accounted of great price in the estimation of those who had the chief control in the criminal department, and should be convinced that similar conduct on his part would lead to promotion.

Sir, criminals are a shrewd race of men, none are quicker in the perception of a sham; and often have I heard from them the remark that the authorities can care little about their reformation while they are intrusted, as they have been, to the management of immoral men. More care, then, is needed in the choice of those who are to be daily with criminals. But while the army is almost the only source whence the officers for criminals are drawn I have little hope of seeing a good moral influence exerted over the criminal class. I would not disparage the morality of the army, but while having been in the army is alone considered the only qualification for an officer over convicts, I despair of seeing any real good done.

Every officer in a prison exerts an influence for good or for evil over the criminals in the prison. How important, then, that the greatest care should be used in their selection. What good can chaplains, religious instructors, and schoolmasters hope to effect if an evil example is afforded by the officers intrusted with the discipline? What reformation can the country look for in its criminal classes until the greatest care is bestowed upon the selection of fit and proper persons to deal with the criminal mind?

A prison, to be reformatory, should be in the hands of men who not only force obedience to its rules, but who, by example and life, testify to criminals that virtue and morality are the atmosphere they breathe.

DELTA.

P.S.—A glance at the prison blue-book shows the military type of the convict prisons—board of directors, a colonel and two captains; governors and deputy-governors of nearly all the prisons, captains, lieutenants and majors; chief warders, pensioners from the army; principal warders, warders, and assistant-warders, mostly from the army.

September 30, 1851.

A WORD FOR THE ADULT CRIMINAL.

To the Editor of the " Daily News."

Sir,—It seems to be the opinion of the press that it is impossible to reform an adult criminal. Those who hold the above opinion point to the various Government plans which have been tried, and have failed. Now, Sir, I am so bold as to assert that, down to the present moment, the Government of this country has never yet adopted, or tried, one single scheme which was in the remotest degree calculated to work out the reformation of adult criminals.

What, you will perhaps say, have we not had legislation upon legislation, and plan upon plan, for the management of criminals ? Yes, we have ; but we have never seen Parliament, nor the Government, adopt a common-sense scheme for the reformation of adult convicts.

Just review the several schemes adopted by Parliament for the treatment of convicts since the period when the colonies of America ceased to be the moral cesspools for the absorption of our vice and guilt. When Government could no longer farm off its criminals, and hide them among the sugar-canes and cotton-plantations, as so many beasts of prey, a receptacle had to be found for them : that receptacle, that moral reformatory, was the hulk. Yes, Sir, Government tried to reform adult convicts by herding them as wild beasts in various convict-hulks in England. It is true, this was said at the time to be only a temporary expedient ; but, like the income-tax and various other bad temporary expedients of Government, it has endured till the present moment ; so that, in the year of our Lord 1856, the whole country has been startled by the atrocities still enacted in one of the hulks.

Our parliamentary Blue-books contain startling and horrifying details, to prove that hulks have never offered nor been adapted to afford the means likely to produce the reformation of adult convicts.

No Government can have cared about the reformation of convicts which confined them in such debasing, such horrible receptacles as are the convict-hulks.

We cannot, therefore, refer to the experiences of the hulk system, and say that the reformation of adult criminals is hopeless, because the treatment they have received therein has failed to bring it about. As well might we hope to cure an ague by causing the patient to inhale the pestilential miasma of a putrid marsh, as to look for the reformation of a convict by placing him for months and years in a convict-hulk. And yet it is a notorious fact, that the greater part of the unreformed convicts who are now the terror and disgrace of the land, have spent years in the soul-polluting atmosphere of our horrible convict-hulks.

Government has tried transportation to penal settlements, and to our various colonies ; but no one will assert that adult convict reformation is hopeless because Norfolk Island and Van Diemen's Land have failed to produce it. The plans there adopted were so contrived that debasement seemed the object, not reformation. We threw masses of criminals upon those distant shores, and left them almost literally without any man to care for their souls. They were permitted to run wild ; and yet we stand aghast, and exclaim, These men are irreclaimable !

It is a fact which will startle Christian men, that shiploads of convicts have left these shores for the Antipodes without the Word of God, excepting such copies as private benevolence bestowed ; and also that they have been left the whole voyage to themselves, without any proper person to give them either moral or religious instruction.   It is true that persons have been appointed to go with each ship, called religious instructors ; but often such persons have needed themselves instruction in the very rudiments of the faith.   I could disclose some startling facts concerning the attainments and morals of several of the so-called religious instructors who have been entrusted with the spiritual care of convicts on their passage to the Antipodes.   I am not now speaking of all : many of them were and are good and holy men, but others have been sent as a matter of convenience and favour, without any care as to their fitness for the duties they were to discharge.   Sir, adult convicts, as far as transportation has been concerned, have never come under a reformatory discipline : hence it cannot be said that transportation has proved them a hopeless class.

We have had model prisons upon the solitary and silent systems.   In those prisons we have deprived numbers of robust adult criminals of their intellects and their health.   And it is no strange result that the silent system was considered hopeless as a means of reformation, when such fearful effects so speedily followed.   But if those systems had been calculated to reform adult convicts, Government determined that all the good they did should be made of no effect, by sending the convicts from their model prisons to their detestable hulks.   I am in a position to know that the excellent treatment of convicts administered by such chaplains as Mr. Reynolds of Wakefield, and Mr. Kingsmill of Pentonville, has resulted in the permanent reformation of numbers who have come under their counsel.   But that model prisons have failed in producing great results, is no wonder ; solitariness and silence are not calculated to reform, unless other judicious measures accompany and follow.   Our model prisons' experiments, therefore, do not prove adult criminals a hopeless class.

But we have Colonel Jebb's improved convict hard-labour establishments, which have in a great measure superseded hulks, and are intended to displace them altogether.   I will do Colonel Jebb the credit to say that his system is a very great improvement upon that of the hulks, but I cannot go so far as to call his system a reformatory one.   His prisons certainly are calculated to prevent the further debasement of their inmates ; but I am at a loss to see how they are, as at present administered, likely to do much in the way of reformation.   It seems to me that Colonel Jebb aims more at making his establishments pay than at making them places to work out the reformation of the convicts.   It is true that he has his chaplains, religious instructors, and schoolmasters ; but if reports which reach me are true, their labours are held secondary, and little account is taken of them.

Sir, will the locking a man in a cell at night, giving him a book to read, forcing him to attend prayers night and morning, *nolens volens,* chapel twice on Sunday, and then placing him all the week in a gang of ruffians, at some employment which in after-life he cannot follow, be likely to reform him ?

Look into our dockyards. You will see a gang of a dozen drawing a cart of chips or a log of timber, or a hundred carrying coals ; and at these employments convicts of all classes labour the whole of their prison term. Is such employment calculated to induce industrious habits in an extravagant man, a pickpocket, &c. ? Is a man likely to be stimulated at such labour ? But think not that I would have all convicts escape this degrading drudgery—they should all pass through it ; but it should only be a preparatory step in a reformatory discipline.

The ticket-of-leave system was well meant, but it has been most carelessly carried out. In fact, Colonel Jebb has more to superintend than mortal man has power or capacity to perform. His ticket-of-leave system could be made a most useful engine in helping forward the reformation of convicts ; but he must become more discriminating in the gift of his tickets—he must adopt more superintendence after the ticket is given—in a word, he must carry out the intentions of the Act of Parliament, before he can hope to realise what I conceive the system is capable of. He must also appoint, to carry on his prison system, men who aim at reformation—he must cease to appoint only because they have held commissions in the army. A person entrusted with the care and control of convicts should be a man of intellect, high morals, and religious ; one who would make it his constant endeavour to improve the wretched beings under his charge—not one who seeks a sinecure, leaving the duties of his office to those beneath him. Officers in the lower grades should be moral men—men whose character would influence more than their uniforms. Then might we expect that Colonel Jebb's prison system would beneficially influence the convicts who come within its pale.

I have attempted to prove that we have not yet tried a reformatory system with our adult criminals. If you will permit me in another letter, I will give you what my ideas of a reformatory system are—its practicability and its economy, when compared with anything yet attempted by the Government of this country.

Sept. 9. CIVIS.

To the Editor of the " Daily News."

Sir,—As you have done me the honour to insert in your impartial paper my plea for adult criminals, in which I endeavoured to show that they have not yet come under a truly reformatory discipline, I shall trespass upon your kindness with another letter, in which I shall attempt to prove that Colonel Jebb's prisons are not reformatories, and also give you what my ideas of a reformatory discipline should be.

First, then, permit me to state why I do not consider the present hardlabour prisons erected under the auspices of Colonel Jebb can be entitled to all the eulogy which he and the directors give them. I am aware, Sir, that my task is somewhat formidable. These prisons are defended by innumerable blue-books ; and I perceive that in Colonel Jebb's last report he endeavours to show that the reformations wrought in his prisons are even more numerous than those of such an establishment as Mettray. Now, Sir, is this anything like a correct representation ? Colonel Jebb says that a given percentage of the Mettray criminals fell ; but he must bear in mind that every Mettray man is known after he leaves, so that if he falls into crime he cannot keep his crime concealed from the knowledge of the authorities of Mettray. But what do Colonel Jebb and the prison directors know of the hundreds and thousands who leave their prisons? Half of them may lead dissolute and vicious lives, and the authorities who sent them forth from prison be none the wiser. So that after the convicts have left his prisons Colonel Jebb can know but little concerning their so-called reformation.

But let us glance a little more narrowly at the reformatory discipline of the Colonel's prisons. We will take Portland, which seems the pet prison. There, the Colonel tells us that it is pleasant to walk through the stone quarries and observe a thousand convicts cheerfully and quietly engaged in that laborious employment. He also points to the Governor's report of the fewness of the prison offences committed by the convicts, and in a somewhat exulting strain point to these facts as a proof of reformation. Now, I am not inclined to underrate these facts. Colonel Jebb deserves the thanks of the community for his admirable prisons, for the discipline he has established, and for the countenance he gives to religious and secular instruction in his prisons. But quietness, apparent cheerfulness, and fewness of prison offences, are not proofs of the reformation of convicts. A very bad man is often a man the most alive to his own interests; and it is a well-known fact to those engaged among convicts that a regular thief and prison-bird is the man who conforms the most to prison rules. And where men come under a semi-military discipline, as the convicts at Portland do, it strikes them at once that it would be folly to attempt to act in opposition to the commands of those who are placed over them, and who have the power to enforce those commands.

But does working in quarries for two, three, or seven years in a quiet and so-called cheerful manner fit a man to return to the bosom of society? Let it be borne in mind that those who work in those stone quarries are compelled to do so; they have no other choice, and the quietness with which they do their work and their apparent cheerfulness are their only chances of getting the least mitigation of their sentence.

Reformation, Sir, does not consist in bringing a man to a mere submission to prison authority, and to the mechanical performance of a certain amount of manual labour, which labour he will never perform after his liberation; and all this too that he may hasten his freedom. If it does, then Colonel Jebb has in a great measure succeeded. But alas! I am too well, far too well, assured of the fact, that from Colonel Jebb's prisons have emanated hundreds and thousands who have not imbibed one single right principle of action; but who have gone forth with the determination to prey upon society for the time to come, as they have done in times past. And why is this? Simply because Colonel Jebb sends them forth from his prisons no better qualified to gain an honest living than when they entered.

Sir, fancy a hundred London or Glasgow thieves working from two to four years in the quarries at Portland, or dragging burdens in the dockyards at Portsmouth or Chatham; have they by such an industrial training learnt to love an honest employment? Grant they have; but you must have a credulous mind to believe it. You send them back to London, or to Glasgow: where, in either place, will they find the stone-quarries to work, or the dockyards in which to labour ? Sir, it is simply absurd to suppose that a thief will be fitted to cease from thieving in London or Glasgow because he has spent four years in, to him, profitless drudgery at Portland or Portsmouth.

To reform a thief, you must get him to love honest labour ; but what labour is there in Colonel Jebb's system a thief is likely to admire ? I can tell you, Sir, that hundreds are habitual thieves because there is nothing else they can turn their hands to. I have held intimate converse with many hundreds of thieves, and I have found that the great majority of them would gladly leave their thieving if you could put them in the way of earning an honest living by labour suitable to their tastes. But is it not preposterous to suppose that hewing stone, dragging burdens, and carrying coals, are employments likely to meet the tastes of men who have spent a life in crime ?

The Government prisons might be made most excellent reformatories at the same expense as at present, but they must be managed on quite a different plan. In the first place, more care must be bestowed in the selection of both superior and inferior officers. Men who throw their energies into the work, and not dilettante governors, are wanted. The inferior officers should also be drawn from among a more moral class of society than are the great majority of the present prison warders. Education in fact, not in theory, should be afforded. And then care should be taken to give a thief an opportunity to learn some useful trade during the time he is an inmate of the prison.

The following, Sir, would be my suggestion :—Let the first stage be some few months at the present uniform drudgery ; let each man, by good conduct and attention to his own mental improvement, by attending a voluntary school in the prison after working hours, earn his discharge from the penal drudgery : and then let the second stage be working at some trade he would wish to learn, under proper trade instructors ; let his improvement in his trade and his industry, coupled with mental improvement, gain for him a mitigation of sentence, so that he might get a ticket-of-leave, work being first obtained for him—this being his third stage ; he remaining the whole period under the supervision of the authorities. I would thus let every convict have the chance of earning his way out of prison by his industry and improvement mentally. This, Sir, might easily be done ; and the economy of the plan would be great. We should thus turn out men capable of earning a living ; and their willingness to do so would be, in a great measure, attested before they left the prison. Colonel Jebb's prisons would be admirably adapted, and a very little additional machinery is needed. Sir, I am confident that convicts might thus become self-supporting, instead of the expense they now are. The plan is carried out nearly in the Reformatory at Smith Street, Westminster. And that thieves are willing to reform, the experience of that establishment must attest ; that adult criminals are capable of reformation, the success of that admirable institution abundantly confirms. I hope the attention of Colonel Jebb and the Home Secretary will be drawn to this subject. The reformation which Colonel Jebb now boasts of in his reports is most fallacious. His prisons, as machines, are a vast improvement upon the hulks ; but he must not look to mere discipline, and imagine that quietness and order, enforced as they are by an iron rule, betoken a reformation of character. His prisons develop none of the better principles of human nature, neither do they afford a criminal a test of his own improvement. His system is the mechanism of the army. As a machine, it works admirably to the eye; but individually, as far as the convicts are concerned, but little real good is done. A man may spend a life in his prisons, and he will have no stimulus to improve himself any further than to keep out of the prison books as a bad prisoner, and thus get home as soon as his fellows.

Our criminal population must have more attention. Transportation cannot drain off our vice any longer; we must, therefore, at once adopt such plans as common sense and philanthropy suggest. Let us no longer shift off the duty by saying adult criminals are hopeless for reformation. Can we despair of their reformation when, in the present century, an island of cannibals has been changed into an island of civilised men? Sir, I for one believe that we can reform the great mass of our adult criminals, if we bring them within the influence of a truly reformatory system; and, in conclusion, I will remark that it is far better to expend a large sum in changing them from rogues into honest men, than to expend millions in looking after and prosecuting them in courts of law.

Thanking you for your indulgence in permitting me a place in your columns, I am, &c.,   CIVIS.

Such were my expressed views of Sir. J. Jebb's system in 1856, two years before I left the convict service, when I was in daily communication with the poor men left to him to reform. Since that time I have learnt more of its abuses, more of its horrors, seen more of its demoralising effects, and how utterly hopeless it is for the country to look for the reformation of convicts, while they are left under the control of Sir. J. Jebb.

The question naturally arises; what is wrong in the system of Sir. J. Jebb? All is wrong. The Board of Directors is a myth,—there is no Board,—Sir. J. Jebb is the Board, his two directors are merely toys in his hands.

The inspection of prisons is a great sham; in fact, the directors know but little more by going to the prisons, than if they stayed in town. What inspection is that, which always apprises the governors, &c., that at such a day, and such an hour, the director will be in the prison?

The convict officials as a body are very immoral men. Drunkenness is a common vice among the warders; they are mostly old soldiers, and I never came acquainted with more immoral men than those I have known placed as warders over convicts.

The warders now supplied to the prisons, in respectability, civil fitness, and morality, are infinitely below the standing of the men who formerly carried on the much decried and horrid system at the hulks. I am not now condemning all, but I am the majority. The following quotation is from the letter just published, written by the Deputy-Governor of Chatham Prison, pp. 13 & 14:—

IMMORALITY OF PRISON WARDERS.

An industrious soldier appears almost a contradiction in terms ; and he was certainly never dreamt of, save by Sir Joshua Jebb, as the model moral reformer. Non-commissioned officers have certainly acquired habits of command ; but in a purely external system, beyond which it is often difficult for them to look. I have known many very admirable exceptions ; but they leave my conviction unshaken, that the school of military discipline is not necessarily the best or only source from which good prison officers can be derived ; and it should not be forgotten that discipline is, after all, only a prison means, while change of character is the great public end. Discharged convicts are not kept all their lives under the restraint of a specially severe code of laws, such as is essential in the army ; but they are expected to exercise individual self-government on their liberation. Supposing a man, therefore, from violent temper, to be addicted to offences against the person on every occasion of annoyance or quarrel, is he likely to learn forbearance or meek submission to injuries, real or imaginary, from one who is imbued with a spirit of personal bravery, directed as it has been in the life of a soldier ?

Sir Joshua Jebb himself makes the following important admissions in one of his circulars to his prison officers :—

" It has, however, been stated by those who take a deep interest in the reformation of convicts (which it must be remembered is one of the essential objects contemplated by Government), that though it may be inferred from the Rules that every officer is required, both by precept and example, to be a moral agent among the prisoners, yet the army not being a good school for the formation of habits fitting them for such duties, an effort should be made, even at a sacrifice, to obtain a class of officers of higher moral qualifications. Now this argument I cannot meet, unless the old soldiers whom I have recommended for the situations they occupy will stand by me, and show that, notwithstanding the disadvantages to which they may have been exposed in early life, they have acquired and possess a just feeling of their responsibilities, and can be as good moral agents, and carry out the duties as well as others."

Whatever may be the meaning of the officers "standing by " Sir Joshua Jebb, it appears difficult to comprehend by what exact process prison warders of inferior intelligence and of the lowest level of education and moral feeling can perform such an act of self-transformation in obedience to an order ; while of the aptitude of the "hardy veterans," as Sir. J. Jebb elsewhere calls them, "who could produce gratifying testimonials of the good opinion of those under whom they had served, and of gallantry and intelligence," for the office of moral reformers, some idea may be formed from the fact that out of the lowest classes of officers at Chatham Prison, numbering not more than a hundred men, there have been dismissed for neglect of duty and insubordination since the opening of the prison, a period of four years, no less than 54, besides compulsory resignations, of which 16 were dismissed for drunkenness on duty. The appointment of an assistant-warder is worth, with gratuity and working pay, about £70 per annum ; and it is essential that, by a system of proper test and examination, men of much superior calibre should be obtained than even many of those who contrive to hold on in the service. That they can be got, if not sought in too narrow a circle, I am convinced; but Sir Joshua Jebb seems pertinaciously to maintain the idea that candidates must necessarily divide themselves into the "hardy veteran" and "the pleasing young man, who would never acquire the habit of command."

I would that the immorality of the convict officers ended with the warders; but Sir. J. Jebb has appointed as governors of his prisons, and deputy governors, and chief warders, men who had not a single intellectual qualification for this office, but who were entirely unfitted, by immorality and vice; not to say anything about appointing them in contravention of the prison rules, when in a state of insolvency. I personally knew the following governors, &c., and can prove the following facts with regard to their fitness for their office. The first was Mr. L——, he had in the prison at one time a woman with whom he cohabited, his wife being there also. This man used to borrow money of the warders, and the convicts were allowed a perfect license; in 1848, he decamped with Government money, and afterwards was taken and transported, and served his time as a convict at Portland. With him was a steward who was accused of embezzlement, and turned out of his stewardship.

The next governor with whom I became acquainted had an idea that convicts must be treated as wild beasts; his name Mr. L. T——. He kept the prison in a furious tempest, he quarrelled with his officers, roused to open revolt the convicts, had furious contests with the chaplain, and ultimately Sir G. Grey had to put him out.

The next I knew was a Captain; he had repeated riots in his prison, absented himself from his charge, held intrigues with the daughter of his warder, and, at last, had to resign, because he was behind with his accounts.

The next was the notorious Major S——. This man kept the convicts, by his crimes and management, in constant revolt, and ultimately figured in the *Police Gazette* as an absconder with £500 government money; although Sir J. Jebb told your Lordships and the Commons that he had resigned his governorship.

The next is Captain B——, who was, until a few weeks since, governor at Chatham. Sir G. Lewis has found it needful to dismiss him. Why? He has been advertised in the *Trades' Protection Gazette* as a gentleman not to be trusted. He kept the prison in permanent discord, was always at war with Major Stewart,* his deputy, and with Mr. Marsh, the chaplain.

There is another governor, whom the chaplain serving with him *reproved* for immoral intrigue with his warder's daughter. The chaplain had the prison made too hot for him by the friend of the

---

* This gentleman has published a letter to Sir J. Jebb, accusing him of injustice, and his system of being a great failure and a sham.

governor, Sir J. Jebb, and had to exchange with another chaplain.

In another prison, at this time, there is a governor who has had one prison ship burnt and destroyed by the convicts under him ; who, by his unwarrantable treatment in another prison, drove the whole body of them into furious outbreak, and who is a man without one attribute for the command of convicts. In the same prison, under him, is a deputy-governor, who has been proved by a chaplain, two religious instructors, and a schoolmaster, guilty of outrageous drunkenness in his prison on the Sabbath-day, which riot was heard by all the convicts. This was proved before Mr. Hall, the magistrate of Bow Street. *In the same prison is a chief clerk, who was steward at Dartmoor, and, when there, embezzled his money to a large amount—was turned out of his office for his theft. Afterwards, as a proof of Sir J. Jebb's opinion of the fitness of things,* he made this unjust steward, what ? Yes, my Lords and Gentlemen, what did Sir J. Jebb think this man's qualifications fitted him for ? Nothing less than to be the religious instructor, the spiritual adviser of 400 convicts. Start not; such is a solemn fact. He sent him off to go to Australia, the only spiritual instructor of 400 convicts on the voyage. But this moral man's fitness for his office disgusted the officers and captain of the ship between Gravesend and Portsmouth, and there he was put ashore ; and there the 400 convicts lost this excellent moral and religious trainer. This man has figured in his old calling, since that time, under the command of Major S——; and yet Sir J. Jebb fosters him with the fondness of a kind father !

Sir J. Jebb has sent, to my knowledge, two other men out with a ship-load of convicts to Australia, to act as religious instructors on the voyage. One, who was obliged to fly his country through debt, and never did, as he said he never would, read prayers or instruct the convicts on the voyage !

Another was a Mr. P——, whom I knew personally, as he was compounder of medicine in the same prison. This man was openly a derider of religion—almost, if not quite a sceptic. He became a ruined man, and wished to get to the colony. Sir J. Jebb made him religious instructor to 400 convicts on the voyage. Such and such prove what Sir Joshua thinks of religion for convicts.

In the same prison above referred to is a chief warder whom Sir G. Grey dismissed for theft and repeated drunkenness, and whom Sir Joshua is pleased to honour. Such, my Lords and Gentlemen, are specimens of the men whom Sir Joshua keeps to train in habits of industry, honesty, and piety, and by whom the convicts are driven to revolt.

Speaking of the notorious Major S—— I must not omit an incident which is almost too dreadful for credence, but alas too true. A warder named Douglas under him had been guilty of a breach of rules, by bringing in tobacco and money for convicts. Major S—— was not content to get against him a conviction for misdemeanour, but he determined to make it forgery, and charged him with writing a letter, and forging the convict's name. The convict Collett had the letter written, and gave it to the warder to get him in the money. When the warder Douglas was charged with the crime before the magistrates, the convict Collett would not swear against him. The magistrates, however, on the evidence of Major S——, &c., committed Douglas to Winchester for trial. In the meantime, the manager of convicts sent down to the prison the pardon of Collett, but he was not presented with it, though Major S—— and the Steward, a Mr. M—— let him know it was there. Collett, the day before the trial came on, told the Author that he would never swear against the warder Douglas. I tried to impress upon him the sin of perjury, and told him his duty was to state the truth, whether for or against the warder. On the morning of the trial, Collett was conveyed to Winchester; he was dressed in a new suit of clothes, given to convicts on their pardon being granted; but his pardon was withheld, and he was told unless he swore against Collett he would be taken back to the prison and his pardon withheld! He did swear, and most falsely that he never gave the warder the letter to get the money—when the convict who wrote the letter for him came forward and owned it. A conviction by the basest perjury was obtained against the misguided, but, as far as forgery was concerned, innocent warder. The result was, in a few weeks after his sentence of transportation his heart broke, and he died. And by the fearful doings of Major S——, the governor, &c., a man was judicially murdered and the soul of a convict blackened with perjury.

I represented all these facts to the chaplain of the prison at the time, but he was a great friend of the worthy Major S——, and would do nothing to get the warder released from the horrid pit into which villany had entrapped him.

Such, my Lords and Gentlemen, are the men whom the Inspector General has appointed to reform convicts ! Men over whom, until this hour, he throws his shield to hide their crimes.

I have adduced enough to prove that the convicts are entrusted to immoral men, and that this system can work nothing but mischief for the convicts, and increase instead of lessen immorality and crime.

I shall now present to your Lordships a more fearful picture still, which will account for the failure of the system upheld by your Director General of Prisons.

Sir Joshua Jebb has been permitted, by the negligence or the complicity of the late Home Secretary, Sir G. Grey, to turn solemn courts of inquiry, instituted in the name of her Majesty, to inquire into the results of his system, and the crimes of his governors, deputy-governors, &c., into fearful courts of oppression and persecution.

My Lords and Gentlemen,—I grieve to bring before your notice the evil deeds of one who has but recently received from the hands of the Queen the honour of knighthood; but the truth must be told, and the guilty must be known, that the innocent may be relieved from a burden of cruel and intolerable oppression.

Sir J. Jebb has so perverted the courts of inquiry into the abuses of his prisons, that every officer now in the service knows that he dares not give truthful evidence before them, unless he is fully prepared to leave the convict service immediately after. Facts—terrible facts, but solemn facts—alone shall prove this charge against Sir J. Jebb; and here I shall trouble your Lordships and Gentlemen to ask for documents, safely but secretly kept at the Home Office, the substance of which I shall now place before you.

In the year 1856, Mr. Roebuck, M.P., called the attention of Sir G. Grey to the condition of the Invalid Convict Prison at Gosport. Sir G. Grey sent down a Commission, composed of Mr. Perry, prison inspector, and Dr. Arnott. They sat at Gosport several days: they called before them a great number of the convicts; then the chaplain, the author, the religious instructor, the schoolmaster, and the principal warder, with many of the warders. They learnt that the sin of Sodom and Gommorrha was rife in the prison—they learnt that drunkenness was common among officers and convicts—they learnt that the convicts were driven to revolt, and to murder the assistant-surgeon, through the cruelty and neglect of the surgeon-superintendent, who had driven *dying* convicts from his surgery, calling them d——d scoundrels, and sent them to work in the dockyard when within a few hours of death, &c., &c.

They learnt that the governor had permitted the convicts to be fed constantly upon unwholesome food; that he was in the habit of borrowing money, &c., from the contractors who supplied the prison —they learnt that he was a defaulter in his accounts; that his management of the prison was sometimes cruel in the extreme to the convicts, while at the same time perfect laxness of discipline constantly prevailed—they learnt that Government stores had been passed out of the prison by steward and governor, to pay their debts, &c., &c.

They learnt that the chief warder was in the habit of appropriating the Government stores, and constantly on duty drunk— they learnt that the deputy-governor was grossly unfit for his post, &c. In a word, my Lords, they reported to the Home Secretary that nothing could be worse than the condition of that prison, which was an establishment founded, officered, and regulated entirely by Sir J. Jebb. They reported to the Home Secretary that the prison had been grossly neglected; that it had not been properly inspected; that it had been kept without sufficient officers; and that the convicts had been grossly neglected. In a word, they told Sir G. Grey that nothing could be worse than the condition and management of that prison.

Sir G. Grey made known the report of the Commissioners to the Chairman and Directors of Convicts. They *disputed the facts*, and were *allowed by Sir G. Grey to hold another commission*, upon the truth of the report of Messrs. Perry and Arnott. Captain O'Brien, Captain Gambier, and Captain Whitty were the second commission. They had the report of the first for their guidance. The author, having been the principal evidence before the first court, was virtually put upon his trial by the second court, and had to substantiate all the evidence he gave before Messrs. Perry and Arnott. The result was, the governor (Major Shaw) absconded during the inquiry, although he had the privilege of putting the author under a searching cross-examination by a solicitor. In six weeks after this the following paragraph appeared in the *Hue and Cry*, June 6, 1856:—"Absconded from Portsmouth, on the 26th ultimo, John Shaw, *alias* Major Shaw, late governor of the *Stirling Castle* hulk, charged with embezzling £500, the monies of her Majesty's Government. The said John Shaw was formerly in the Spanish Legion, and has also held the appointment of superintendent in the City of London and Birmingham police : is supposed to have some property in Ireland. Description : About 55 years of age, 6ft. 1in. high, prominent nose, &c.; rough in his manner and address, &c. ; has friends in Dublin," &c. Reward—Nothing ! ! ! Consequently he has not been taken, although seen in London since.

Mark, my Lords and Gentlemen, this notice was issued six weeks after the crime was proved the second time. But Sir J. Jebb, in his Blue Book for that year, has told you this worthy man resigned, and has said nothing of the crimes he committed; upon which the *Morning Star* thus comments :—

BLUE BOOK ACCURACY.—A correspondent writes :—The " Blue Book " on convict prisons for the year 1856, published in August, 1857, under " Hulk Establishments," p. 370, states that the late governor of the convict hulks resigned his appointment, whereas the said governor is advertised in the *Police Gazette* of June 6, 1856, as having absconded with £500, the monies of her Majesty's Government, &c. It is scarcely credible to think that these two contrary statements both emanate from sources of public authority, or that the report to Sir George Grey in the " Blue Book " can pretend to furnish authentic information to Parliament.

After the second commission failed to white-wash the friends of Sir J. Jebb, or to gainsay the report of the first commission, Sir G. Grey ordered the dismissal of several officers, among them the surgeon-superintendent, a chief warder, steward, &c., &c. But Sir J. Jebb, after this dismissal was signed and delivered to them, threw around them his all-powerful mantle, and not one of them has ever left the service a single day, nor suffered one iota for their great crimes. The reason is obvious ; Sir J. Jebb had sagacity enough to see that he could not suffer the least criminals to be punished, when the report of the commission brought home the chief blame of all to him.

The surgeon-superintendent, knowing this, pointedly told Sir Joshua as much, and Sir Joshua being omnipotent in the convict service, set aside the solemn acts of Sir G. Grey; and, because he was not prepared to take his own share of the guilt for all the horrors of that fearful prison, he has kept in the convict service men doubly proved guilty of great immorality and crime.

But this line of conduct entailed upon Sir Joshua proceedings even more atrocious; if he *must defend and foster the guilty*, then he must persecute and sacrifice *the innocent*. Hear it, ye Lords and Commons of England! Sir J. Jebb has dared to make the innocent suffer for the guilty. He has, in your name, and under your authority, driven from the convict service gentlemen and officers for no other crime than proving him guilty of gross neglect of duty, and for exposing the crimes of his officers, when asked so to do.

When Messrs. Perry and Arnott held their inquiry, they told the officers that no harm could or should befall them if they revealed the truth. Moreover, they assured the writer of this letter, that his name or what he revealed should not be known. Instead of that, the writer stood a two days' trial upon his evidence before them—proved it all—but has been driven forth upon the world, at a great loss, by Sir J. Jebb, because he dared to be honest and truthful.

Each of the principal witnesses upon the commission has been discharged or pensioned off by Sir J. Jebb, while others have been subjected to constant persecution. These are the Rev. J. K. Walpole, chaplain; William Thwaites, 1st schoolmaster; Mr. Dunkinson, principal warder, pensioned; Mr. Greve, principal warder, pensioned, both strong and young, and able men; Mr. Lake, religious instructor, persecuted; Mr. Bevis, religious instructor, the same.

Sir J. Jebb appointed a new governor in the place of the runway Major Shaw, a Captain Warren. Before he sent him to the prison, he was shown the evidence given by the officers in the prison he was to govern; and the author of this has read a letter from Sir J. Jebb, in which he tells Captain Warren that the author and other officers would give him more trouble than the convicts. Captain Warren acted upon the wishes of Sir J. Jebb, and lent himself to get the chaplain, and Mr. Thwaites, especially, out of the service. Mr. Thwaites was particularly obnoxious to Sir J. Jebb, from his fearlessness, his candour, and his truthfulness. Mr. Thwaites suffered repeated insults and oppressions from Captain Warren, who was secretly upheld in all this by Sir J. Jebb, until he could bear it no longer, when he appealed to the Home Secretary against the governor and his deputy. Mr. Thwaites made his charges against them, the whole of which were solemnly attested by the Rev. J. K. Walpole, the religious instructor, and Mr. Bevis, schoolmaster. Mr. Thwaites should have been supported by the Rev. W. G. Cookesley, formerly of Eton, who unfortunately was not present when Mr. Hall, of Bow-street, made his, what proved a mock inquiry.

Sir J. Jebb, who wanted to be the judge in the matter, flagrantly took the side of the accused, telegraphed to the prison that he was coming as a witness against Mr. Thwaites, and thus intimidated the officers whom Mr. Thwaites intended to have called. He also removed from the prison, pending the inquiry, the convicts material for the case, and, when the inquiry was over, returned them ; a matter so flagrant, that Mr. Thwaites holds a letter from Sir G. Grey, dated 19th January, 1858, saying that it ought not to have been, and should be strictly inquired into, but it never has.

The following documents will prove that Mr. Thwaites has sought redress by private efforts, and that he has striven to keep so foul an injustice, and such a magnitude of guilt from being the scandal of the convict system.

Mr. Thwaites has had interviews with several members of Parliament, some of whom promised him to bring the matter forward—Mr. Roebuck among the number—Mr. Milner Gibson told Mr. Thwaites that he ought not to rest until he obtained justice, and promised himself to do what he could to get it for him.

The following statement has been printed and circulated in high quarters, but with no permanent result :—

Statement of the case of WILLIAM THWAITES, late schoolmaster at Lewes convict prison, alleged to have been improperly dismissed in December, 1857, in consequence of his having given evidence inculpatory of officials of the prison, and of its management.

In 1856, a complaint was made to Mr. Roebuck, M.P., of the state and management of H. M. convict hulk *Stirling Castle*, at Gosport, and he procured from Sir George Grey, then Home Secretary, a commission of inquiry, composed of Mr. Perry, a Prison Inspector, and Dr. Arnott.

Shortly after Messrs. Perry and Arnott had entered upon their duties, they sent for Mr. Thwaites, and told him that they found it difficult to come at the truth, and had been informed he could give them the required information. They further stated he should receive no injury on account of the evidence he gave. He then expressed his readiness to tell them all he knew, as he had long been anxious to see an amendment in the condition and management of the hulk.

The following are the principal points of Mr. Thwaites's evidence :—

1st.—That the convicts were in a demoralised state, and without discipline ; in fact, that he had seen several of them in a state of intoxication in the prison ; and drinking and smoking, although strictly prohibited, as well as fighting and swearing, were commonly practised among them.

2nd.—That some of the superior officers had been in a state of intoxication when on duty amongst the convicts.

3rd.—That the food supplied to the convicts was bad in quality, of which they had repeatedly complained.

4th.—That the convicts stated that they could get no attention to their complaints, and that the governor prevented them from seeing the visiting director, and punished them if they complained.

5th.—That the convicts complained that they were hindered in getting their liberty by the governor : alleging that he had not the funds to pay the expenses allowed by the country ; that this was a fact known to all in the ship.

6th.—That the governor had laid himself under obligations to the provision contractors by borrowing money of them, so that food, which was unfit for consumption, was received in the prison.

7th.—That the governor and steward were in the habit of passing Government stores out of the ship to pay their debts with, and that tradesmen had to summon them to the County Court to get the money owing to them from the Government.

8th.—That convicts were sent out of the hulk without the clothes which ought to have been allowed them, the clothing being detained at Gosport for the carriage owing to the railway.

9th.—That the *Stirling Castle* hulk had always been insufficiently supplied with officers.

10th.—That so fearful had the state of the ship become, a number of the convicts had banded themselves together to murder some of the superior officers, that attention might be drawn to the state of the ship, and redress obtained to their grievances ; and in pursuance of this plot, Assistant Surgeon Chas. Hope was *murdered* in February, 1856, by convict Jones, one of this band.

The Rev. J. K. Walpole, who was chaplain in the prison at the time, endeavoured to save the life of Jones, because of the frightful state of the prison, which had led to the murder ; and to use the language of the convicts themselves, " they were treated more like beasts than men, and would sooner be out of life than remain in it."

11th.—That the habit of swearing was one continually practised by the governor, and, in fact, that profanity was the atmosphere of the prison.

12th.—That sick convicts had been left without proper medical attention, and put to work in the dockyard when within a few hours of their death.

13th.—That unnatural crimes had been alleged to have been committed in the hulk.

14th.—That the ship with upwards of 400 convicts had been left without a regular chaplain for nine months, his duties having been principally thrown upon Mr. Thwaites ; and that there was only one schoolmaster during fourteen months, three being the proper number for 400 convicts.

When the Commissioners asked what parties Mr. Thwaites blamed for this state of things, he answered—the directors in London, whose duty it was to exercise a proper supervision and control, which had been neglected.

On account of the improper conduct thus brought to the notice of the Secretary of State, the deputy-governor and the steward, the chief warder, and a principal warder were removed, and dismissed, although afterwards restored.

Evidence was given by the Rev. J. K. Walpole, chaplain; Mr. William Lake, religious instructor; Mr. John Bevis, schoolmaster; Messrs. Dunkinson and Scott, principal warders; Mr. John Greve, warder, and many others; but it is complained that these charges were hushed up, that the delinquents escaped proper punishment; whilst those who thus did their duty to the country by telling unpalatable truths were visited with persecution and disgrace.

When Messrs. Perry and Arnott sent in their report, it was denied by the prison directors. Sir George Grey thereupon granted another inquiry in order to allow the authorities of the hulk an opportunity of disproving what was alleged against them, as to the state and management of the hulk.

The second commission was composed of Captains O'Brien and Whitty, prison directors, who had the management of the hulk, and Captain Gambier, then governor of Millbank, but now a prison director. Mr. Thwaites was again examined, his evidence being thoroughly sifted by the governor and his solicitor, but his statements remained unshaken; and during the examination, Major Shaw, the governor, absconded with £500 of Government money, and though advertised in the *Hue and Cry*, was afterwards represented in the official accounts as having resigned his situation.

In consequence of this commission, the medical superintendent was required to resign, and refused, upon which his dismissal was sent to him, and his appointment offered to another surgeon: he thereupon went to Colonel Jebb, threatening that he would have a court-martial, and thus prove that he only acted under orders; whereupon he was permitted to resume his position, his dismissal being cancelled.

Several other officers of the prison, against whom improper conduct had been proved, were only removed to other prisons, and are now in the service.

Such were all the results of these two solemn inquiries.

When Captain Warren, the new governor, was appointed, the evidence was shown to him, and Mr. Thwaites was represented as a dangerous man, who would give more trouble than the convicts.

It was through the influence of Captain Warren, and in consequence of unfounded charges brought by him, that Mr. Thwaites was compelled to ask for further inquiry from Sir G. Grey.

At this inquiry Mr. Thwaites's charges had the support of the late chaplain, the religious instructors, and the other schoolmaster; but he was not supported as he ought to have been by other officers of the prison, who varied from their previous statements, nor had he the evidence of the convicts whom he intended to have called, as they were, previous to the inquiry, removed from the prison, but after the inquiry sent back, a proceeding Sir G. Grey said should be strictly investigated, as a letter from him to Mr. Thwaites, dated 19th of January last, shows; but he, Sir George Grey, left office before the matter was inquired into.

Mr. Thwaites was held not to have established all the charges he had made, and was dismissed.

Mr. Thwaites feels that he has been unjustly condemned and punished in consequence of his endeavours to draw attention to those fearful abuses which were at one time rife in the hulk, and for *no other cause ;* and this he is confident he could establish upon a fair and impartial inquiry, which he now solicits, if he had the unbiassed evidence of the officers of the prison, and also of the convicts who were not produced on the last occasion ; but his chief desire is that a full and complete investigation should be made into the statements he has brought forward of the condition and management of this Government prison, with the view to the correction of such frightful evils.

For this summary dismissal, seriously affecting his character, and doing great and positive injury to his prospects in life, Mr. Thwaites seeks for compensation, if not restoration to an office which he filled for so many years, and, as he trusts, without a stain upon his conduct, his zeal, or his efficiency.

If it were needful to support the character of Mr. Thwaites, who is now a city missionary at Harlesden, beyond the proof of a long service with the Government, a reference is permitted to be made to the Rev. W. G. Cookesley, late master of Eton, now vicar of Pocklington, Yorkshire, who is well acquainted with the circumstances that led to Mr. Thwaites's dismissal, as he was then acting as chaplain at the prison.

WILLIAM THWAITES.
Harlesden Green, Harrow Road, March, 1858.

Voluminous correspondence has taken place between Mr. Thwaites, Sir G. Grey, Sir G. C. Lewis, and Sir J. Jebb, the last portion of which is now presented, with the result.

Copy of a letter sent to Sir G. Grey on July 14, 1859; a copy of which was also sent to the Right Hon. T. M. Gibson, M.P., on the same day ; and afterwards re-copied and sent to the Right Hon. Sir G. C. Lewis, Home Secretary.

Harlesden, July 14, 1859.

Right Hon. Sir,—As you are now again in office, though not the Home Secretary, I feel it my duty to make another appeal to you to right me of that cruel wrong which you, through misrepresentations, were induced to do me when last you were Home Secretary. I am the more emboldened to hope for justice from the fact, that one of your colleagues in the present Cabinet has had the facts laid before him, and spoke to you upon the same, when neither he nor you could have had the least hope of being in your present useful and honourable conjunction.

I appeal to you as a gentleman to do me justice. You did me a *cruel wrong* when you permitted Colonel Jebb to persuade you to lend your name to my dismissal from the Convict Service, in which I did my country and my Queen good service ; and I can challenge Colonel Jebb, or any one who knew me, to deny that I served my country faithfully and well.

Sir George Grey, you allowed me to be dismissed Her Majesty's service because I had the common honesty and the moral courage to report to Her Majesty's Commissioners the *fearful evils* which raged in Her Majesty's Invalid Convict Prison. Right Hon. Sir, it was because of my reporting to Messrs. Perry and Arnott, your Commissioners in 1856, the disgraceful and fearful condition of the Stirling Castle Hulk, that I was hunted from the service and deprived of my pension, which was due in a few weeks from the time of my dismissal.

Right Hon. Sir, the proceedings for which you ostensibly dismissed me, had no more to do with my dismissal than they had with bringing you back into office. Colonel Jebb instructed Captain Warren against me; he even permitted him to read the evidence I gave your Commissioners; and he knew, before he had ever seen me, that to oust me from the Convict Service was the thing of all others that would best please his superior, Colonel Jebb.

I appealed to you against such conduct, but my appeal was futile, as Colonel Jebb *intimidated the officers, removed the convicts,* and has since punished the *officials* who dared to attest *solemnly* to the truth of all *my charges.* I have *indubitable evidence of all these facts.*

But one more extraordinary and terrible fact is in existence, viz., those persons whom you dismissed for their crimes in the Stirling Castle Hulk, Colonel Jebb retained in the service. These are—Dr. ——, Mr. ——, embezzler; Mr. ——, embezzler; Mr. ——, drunkard and thief; Mr. ——,* drunkard; and others against whom foul offences were proved before two solemn commissions—whose crimes you yourself admitted were all proved; while I, who at great personal risk brought these crimes to light at the request of your commissioners, have been hunted out of the service.

Right Hon. Sir, my cause is so just, that I cannot, I will not permit it to slumber—only the accidents of change of Government have prevented it coming before Parliament. But as a Christian, and holding the office I do, I have been advised to make this final appeal to you, to prevent the public scandal which such revelations as I can make would bring upon the Home Department while under your control. I acquit you of all privity to the fearful injustice done me. But I feel that, as you were responsible for all I have unjustly suffered, I have a right to propose to you a plan for bringing to a conclusion the wrong I am suffering.

I am entitled to compensation and my pension. I was a yearly servant, and by law can claim one year's salary; and having served nine years and ten months, I thus, by the year due to me, am entitled to a pension for over ten years' service. I therefore propose that I shall receive one year's salary, and my pension from April 1, 1859.

Colonel Jebb cannot, he dare not, come before the public and answer for the manner in which he has screened publicly-condemned officials, and persecuted those who were the innocent evidence to convict the same. I therefore make this appeal to you, before using those constitutional means which lie in my reach. I shall write to this effect to Milner Gibson, before whom I have laid my case, and whom I asked, before the late dissolution of Parliament, to get for me a Committee of the House of Commons.

I have one other consideration to place before you. I spent nearly ten years of the best portion of my life teaching convicts—nine years of that time with diseased men. My health was ruined while with them.

---

* The names were given in full in this letter.

Through sympathy, I was attacked with dangerous fits, being daily with men subject to the same. I therefore have a claim upon my country for humane treatment; and am certain that the public will never countenance the fearful injustice inflicted upon me, simply for daring to perform a religious duty at the summons of the Queen.

Sir, I hold the highest testimonials of conduct and ability for the whole time I was in the service; and my dismissal has obtained for me the approval and patronage of some of the best men in the land.

I remain, Right Hon. Sir, your obedient servant,
W. THWAITES.

Right Hon. Sir George Grey, M.P., Chancellor
of the Duchy of Lancaster.

Answers of Sir G. Grey—

Eaton Place, July 16th, 1859.

Sir,—I have received your letter of the 14th inst., but I can only refer you to my letter of the 9th of March last, and repeat that any representations you desire to make on the subject of your removal from the convict service should be addressed to the Secretary of State.

I remain, Sir, yours obediently,

Mr. Thwaites. G. GREY.

Letter referred to above—

Eaton Place, March 9th, 1859.

Sir,—I have received your letter of the 8th inst., with reference to your removal from the convict service. As I no longer hold the office of Secretary of State, I cannot interfere any further in the matter. Any representation you desire to make with regard to it should be addressed to the present Secretary of State. I am, Sir, yours obediently,

Mr. Thwaites. G. GREY.

Answer of Sir G. C. Lewis—

Whitehall, July 29th, 1859.

Sir,—I am directed by Secretary Sir George Lewis to acknowledge the receipt of your letter of the 14th inst., respecting your removal from the convict service, and to acquaint you that he must decline to interfere in a matter which has been definitively settled by his predecessors in office.

I am, Sir, your obedient servant,
GEO. CLIVE.

Mr. W. Thwaites, 2 Chapel Terrace, Harlesden, Willesden.

Answer of Milner Gibson—

Board of Trade, Whitehall, July 16th, 1859.

Sir,—I am directed by Mr. Milner Gibson to acknowledge the receipt of your letter; and I am to acquaint you that Mr. Gibson will give the circumstances of your case his best consideration.

I am, Sir, your obedient servant,

Mr. W. Thwaites. HENRY CALCRAFT.

The *Times* has been repeatedly appealed to, but steadily refuses, from some reason best known to the Editor, to insert one word that would call attention to the unjust doings of Sir J. Jebb.

The case of the chaplain is equally unjust and cruel, whose printed statement, I have liberty to make use of, and which, with other documents, and the only letter Sir J. Jebb has ever dared to write, I now place before you.

Statement of the Case of the Rev. J. K. Walpole, late Chaplain in Her Majesty's Convict Service, alleged to have been illegally removed from his office.

The following statement of facts is submitted by Rev. J. K. Walpole to his friends, but with the greatest regret. Having made every other effort, he finds it necessary to ask their protection, to vindicate his character, and to describe the course pursued by the convict authorities to induce the Right Honourable the Home Secretary to remove him from his office of Chaplain in Her Majesty's Convict Service, which was effected by *illegal* means, the proof and scrutiny into which Rev. J. K. Walpole earnestly invites. The motives can be shown to have been connected with private personal resentment against him; and the illegality of the proceeding is increased by the avowal that "a duty to look to the public interests" was the necessary motive for his removal.

1. Rev. J. K. Walpole was removed from the Chaplaincy of Her Majesty's convict invalid hulk, *Defence*, at Woolwich, on December 12th, 1856, which was notified to him by Colonel Jebb, Chairman of the Directors of Convict Prisons, in a letter, delivered by Captain Gambier's hands (See Appendix A), of the same date; and the reason assigned for his removal was, that he had "given so many and such just causes of offence to the superior officers of the ship."

2. Rev. J. K. Walpole denies having given any such "causes of offence;" and it would be found, on proper inquiry, that all proof of his having done so would fail. He affirms that it is he himself who has to complain of various offences, affronts, &c., on the part of the above officers, which he can fully substantiate by evidence.

3. Rev. J. K. Walpole regrets to state that Colonel Jebb has subsequently, in a letter (See Appendix B.) to him of the 22nd December, 1856, denied that it was for "offending the officers" that he was removed from his office, although he did certainly assign that as the reason in his letter of the 12th December, 1856; and that his "colleagues" (Captain O'Brien and Captain Gambier) were "unanimous" with himself that *for this reason* Rev. J. K. Walpole could no longer be retained as Chaplain.

4. Rev. J. K. Walpole regrets also to state that Captain Gambier, Visiting Director, has denied to Rev. J. K. Walpole, in a room full of witnesses, that it was for the above reason he was removed, which induces the painful conclusion that Colonel Jebb and Captain Gambier must have stated that which is not true.

5. Supposing the above charge against Rev. J. K. Walpole to have been true, the sentence pronounced has been excessive, and by far too severe; that a mere transfer to another sphere of duty, of which there are many instances on record, would have been an amply sufficient measure for the alleged offence; that no sentence of publicly-made or publicly-administered law ever yet designed the destruction of the person who came under its influence.

6. The sentence in itself is severe enough, but it is aggravated by the following considerations: Rev. J. K. Walpole being under the legal disabilities of holy orders of the Established Church, is thereby disqualified from receiving many an appointment which would have been open to him as a layman; and having given 20 years of his life to convicts in Australia, on the ocean, and in England, and not having formed any connections out of the convict service, through whom he might obtain a professional position adequate to the support and education of his family, has been reduced to the most distressing circumstances for a clergyman and a gentleman; this being the second winter that himself and his family have thus passed; and he submits that almost under any conceivable circumstances, he would have more than expiated whatever could have been laid against him.

7. Not only is the charge contained in Colonel Jebb's letter of the 12th December, 1856, incapable of being substantiated, as well as various other unfounded and frivolous *since-made* allegations of *previous* offences, which, even if true, must have lapsed on the principle of condonation; but Rev. J. K. Walpole would court public inquiry to discover anything in his moral or professional character or conduct which could have merited so extreme a step.

8. On the contrary, he begs leave to affirm, although he would rather be excused speaking so of himself, that it would be found, on proper inquiry, that it was matter of public notoriety he was courteous and kind to all, efficient in his duties, laborious in the discharge of them, and universally respected by, and acceptable to, the convicts.

9. It is with the utmost pain and reluctance that Rev. J. K. Walpole states, that this unhappy affair has *originated* in personal ill-will on the part of Colonel Jebb against him, which can be proved by documentary evidence; that Captain Gambier has lent himself to the carrying out of Colonel Jebb's design of ejecting Rev. J. K. Walpole from his office, which can be proved; that Captain Warren, governor of the convict invalid establishment, co-operated with the same object, of which there is proof; that the nature of the proceeding has been that of a "conspiracy," having private ends in view, although the "public interests" were assigned as the object; and that thus Rev. J. K. Walpole has been *illegally* removed from his office. In his many fruitless efforts to obtain justice he has bitterly experienced the truth of Cicero's reflection:—"Nullæ sunt occultiores insidiæ," &c. "There are no ill designs more unfathomable than those which are masked under the pretence of duty, or some plea of necessity."

10. Rev. J. K. Walpole would emphatically specify the following transaction, which, as an overt act, must satisfy every candid and honourable mind as to the *animus* entertained against him, and especially as immediately preceding his removal from Her Majesty's service:—That a drunken debauch of a most outrageous nature was enacted on board the *Defence*, convict hulk, at Woolwich, by the deputy-governor and steward, Messrs. Finnie and Whiteman, on a Saturday night in November, 1856, and continued until two o'clock on Sunday morning, which was heard by Rev. J. K. Walpole and others, who can depose to it, and with which he made Colonel Jebb acquainted; that he sent Captain Gambier to Woolwich to inquire into it, who,

without calling on Rev. J. K. Walpole to prove his allegations, and even without his knowledge, made private inquiry of the accused parties as to whether the occurrence had happened, to which a direct denial was given, and a written statement was furnished by them, describing the affair as a convivial but quiet meeting, and that they retired to bed at 12 o'clock; but should these statements be forthcoming in a public inquiry, it would be found that they would be plainly contradicted by the clear and corroborative statements of the witnesses of undoubted veracity, whom Rev. J. K. Walpole can bring forward; that Captain Gambier reported to Colonel Jebb that Rev. J. K. Walpole's statement was untrue; and that not long after Rev. J. K. Walpole was removed for " offending the superior officers of the ship," of whom the deputy-governor and the steward are two.

11. Rev. J. K. Walpole would subjoin to the preceding paragraph for complete explanation.—That Colonel Jebb must admit that he was made aware of a drunken outrage having taken place, and that he clearly understood it as such, and that he sent Captain Gambier to Woolwich to inquire into it; that Captain Gambier must admit having made an inquiry on board the hulk *Defence*, but privately, and without Rev. J. K. Walpole's knowledge, whose statement on the subject he nevertheless informed Colonel Jebb was untrue; that Colonel Jebb must admit that he proceeded to recommend to Sir George Grey to resort to extreme measures with Rev. J. K. Walpole, although aware of the privacy of Captain Gambier's inquiry, from the non-existence of any minutes of evidence to lay before him, which, in accordance with fairness and equity, and all custom, are always prepared with care, where, in any inquiry ,with the *object* of learning the truth, the vital interests of any subject of Her Majesty are involved; being intended to show that the inquiry has been conducted with the public interest in view, and with a fair hearing to all parties concerned. That the deputy-governor and steward must admit that they have owned to a convivial meeting, of which they have given an account; but it can be proved, by the reliable evidence that Rev. J. K. Walpole can bring forward, that they have given a false account; for that they were so utterly intoxicated when they retired to bed at two o'clock on Sunday morning that they could not possibly give any account of themselves at all.

12. Such an occurrence ought not to be allowed to die out without due inquiry. It is a lamentable fact that Her Majesty's officers should thus have disgraced themselves and brought discredit on the service; the deputy-governor especially, he being in sole charge of the convict establishment (the governor not sleeping in it, in disregard of the first section of the printed rules under " Governor," which rigidly enforces that he shall not pass a night out of the prison; and on a subsequent occasion, in a similar absence of the governor, the hulk *Defence* was lost by conflagration off Woolwich Arsenal, while in sole charge of the same deputy-governor) that the officers in general, and the convicts, were awoke by the noises, knowing whence and from whom they proceeded; and that the occurrence was afterwards a subject of common scandal.

13. Rev. J. K. Walpole cannot refrain from observing that the

officers in question are still retained in the convict establishment; the consequences of their offence, as prescribed in the printed rules, which is "dismissal" (General Rules for Officers, Section 10) for the slightest degree of intoxication, having been visited upon himself, the Chaplain.

14. It would be found on inquiry that there have been chaplains, and others, officers of various grades in Her Majesty's convict service, some of whom have been grave offenders, who have not lost their posts, having been permitted to exchange with other officers of like standing in other prison establishments; and which course, if considered necessary that he should leave the scene of his labours, ought by analogy to have been adopted with Rev. J. K. Walpole in preference to his entire removal from Her Majesty's service, with loss not only of his income, but also of prospective pension, which amounts to an enormous fine inflicted without a trial; and, moreover, not one officer implicated in the late *extensive abuses* in the hulks to which Rev. J. K. Walpole was attached has been dismissed.

15. Rev. J. K. Walpole would point out a special case which must convince every candid and honourable mind of great partiality—that of Warder Fraser, of Chatham Convict Prison, who about this time last year having been removed from his situation, as he alleged, unjustly, cut his throat dangerously at Plumstead, after recovering from which he was completely re-instated in his position at Chatham prison. If Warder Fraser had a claim for re-instatement, Rev. J. K. Walpole submits that he has one likewise.

16. There is a feature upon which Rev. J. K. Walpole cannot refrain from stressing most strongly, and he believes, justly, as a subject of Her Majesty, viz., the nature of the tribunal by which he was deprived of his office, and the mode of procedure by which it was effected: the tribunal consisting of three military officers, Colonel Jebb, Captain O'Brien, and Captain Gambier (one of whom, Captain Gambier, having conducted the private inquiry at Woolwich, being both accuser and one of the judges), sitting in close court, and without giving the chaplain a hearing, deciding on *ex parte* statements in favour of the officers of the hulk, two of whom had been also in the army; thus furnishing an example of hasty justice, which, from their professional career, they must have known is not customary even in the army, and which ought not to have been applied to an ordained minister of God. Rev. J. K. Walpole cannot believe that the Right Hon. the Home Secretary will leave unredressed a sentence of such excessive severity, proceeding from a tribunal so constituted, and being a standing department of the Home Office, with vast patronage and unbounded influence, thus giving no hope of escape to any person obnoxious to them.

17. Rev. J. K. Walpole would also mention another ground of complaint, which he believes will be allowed to be a just one—that he has been publicly and unjustly stigmatized in the "Report on Convict Prisons, for 1856," made to Sir George Grey, by Colonel Jebb and Captain Gambier, and "presented to both Houses of Parliament by command of Her Majesty," where (page 371) it is stated that "Rev. J. K. Walpole's services have been dispensed with late in the year," and that therefore no chaplain's report for the year was available for

publication, whereas he could, and would, have supplied one if required. Rev. J. K. Walpole remarks the more strongly on the unfairness with which his name has been thus publicly treated, in contrast with the favour shown to the late governor of the hulks, Major Shaw, who in the same report (page 370) is mentioned as having "resigned" his appointment, while he was advertised in the "*Police Gazette*, of June 6th, 1856," as having "absconded from the hulks with £500, the monies of Her Majesty's Government," &c., &c.

18. Rev. J. K. Walpole assures his friends that with the evidence he can produce, he can prove that he has very just grounds of complaint. As the hulks were in a most demoralized condition, both among officers and convicts, through conscientiously endeavouring to bring this state of things under Sir George Grey's own personal notice, he incurred Colonel Jebb's resentment, which was evinced in many ways, ending in his removal after Captain Gambier's private inquiry at Woolwich; and for the truth of what he asserts he appeals to the consciences of the above two gentlemen, feeling sure they will not contradict him, nor that they will repudiate the whole responsibility of past unhappy occurrences connected with the Convict Invalid Establishment.

19. In conclusion, Rev. J. K. Walpole has, since his removal, written at large, explaining what ever required explanation, pointing out the injustice that has been done, and the sufferings inflicted, and imploring a re-consideration of the case, but unsuccessfully: still he confidently trusts, that in consideration of the preceding statement of the illegal mode of his removal from his office, and the wrongs and sufferings he has undergone, Her Majesty's Home Secretary will yet see reason to indemnify him, by re-instatement in Her Majesty's convict service.

J. K. WALPOLE,
Late chaplain in Her Majesty's convict service.

Plumstead, Kent, April 9, 1858.

Appendix A, referred to in paragraph 1.

Extract verbatim from Colonel Jebb's letter of the 12th December, 1856, to Rev. J. K. Walpole, informing him of his removal, and assigning the reason for it:—

45 Parliament Street, 12th December, 1856.

Sir,—   *   *   *   *

I have now to inform you that, having consulted my colleagues, we are unanimously of opinion that it is a duty to look to the public interests, and that they cannot fail to be prejudiced by the continuance of any one in the execution of the important duties of chaplain, who has given the superior officers of the ship so many and such just causes of offence. We are therefore of opinion that it will be most for the interests of the service to make temporary provision for the discharge of those duties, and to release you from further attendance and responsibility.

*   *   *   *   *

I am, Sir,
Your obedient Servant,

The Rev. J. K. Walpole,   (Signed)   J. JEBB.
&c., &c., &c.

Appendix B, referred to in paragraph 3.

Extract verbatim from Colonel Jebb's letter of the 22nd December, 1856, to Rev. J. K. Walpole:—

45 Parliament Street, 22nd December, 1856.

Reverend Sir,—   *   *   *   *

With respect to your saying that I have advised Sir George Grey to turn you and your family into the world in the middle of winter for " offending the superior officers of the ship"—that may be the light in which you may choose to view and represent the circumstances; but I can only say you are entirely in error on both points.

   *   *   *   *   *

I am, Reverend Sir,
Your obedient Servant,

The Rev. J. K. Walpole, &c., &c.   (Signed)   J. JEBB.

The following petition has been transmitted to a Member of Parliament, for presentation to the House of Commons —

To the Honourable the House of Commons of the United Kingdom, in Parliament assembled:

The humble petition of the Reverend Joseph Kidd Walpole, late chaplain in Her Majesty's convict service, sheweth,

1. That your petitioner was chaplain of the *Defence*, convict hulk, at Woolwich, up to December 12th, 1856, when he was dismissed from his office, because—as he was informed in a letter of the above date, from Colonel Jebb, Chairman of Directors of Convict Prisons,—he had " given so many and such just causes of offence to the superior officers of the ship." (*See Appendix.*)

II. That your petitioner respectfully denies that he ever gave any such causes of offence; and he solemnly assures your honourable House, that they could not be proved in a fair and open inquiry, which he most earnestly implores your honourable House to grant him.

III. That your petitioner would draw the attention of your honourable House to the fact, that he did affirm, in writing, to Colonel Jebb, that the Deputy Governor of the *Defence*, Mr. Finnie, and the steward, Mr. Whiteman, " superior officers," had enacted, on a Saturday night, and until two o'clock on the ensuing Sabbath morning, a drunken debauch, which was of the most outrageous nature conceivable, which was heard by your petitioner, and by two officers, who can depose to it even upon oath.

IV. That instead of your petitioner being called upon to prove so grave a charge, affecting the honour, and discipline, and morals of Her Majesty's convict service, the visiting director, Captain Gambier, held a private inquiry upon it, unknown at the time to your petitioner, by which it was settled, on the representations given by the guilty parties; that your petitioner's statement was untrue, and, shortly afterwards, your petitioner was dismissed. That the production of the minutes and other documents connected with this inquiry, would show that it was held unknown to your petitioner.

V. That your petitioner would consider the preceding a sufficient specimen of the unfairness of which he has such just grounds to complain; and begs permission to affirm that no other offences alleged to have been given by him would be found to have any better foundation in truth than the preceding.

VI. That the establishment to which your petitioner was attached, having been for a long time in a state of desperate and murderous insubordination, through the extreme unfitness of the officers, your petitioner gave offence by attempting to bring this state of things before the personal knowledge of the highest authority, the ultimate result of which has been his dismissal, as before stated.

VII. That your petitioner humbly submits that, having been absolutely dismissed for the cause assigned, and being in effect fined in the loss of his income and prospective pension, without any trial, or opportunity of self-defence, or explanation, he has been punished excessively. That it would be found he has been the victim of a conspiracy, and therefore punished illegally.

VIII. That your petitioner having given the best years of his life to convicts, has not formed even the usual curate's connections, with a view to future preferment, and has a large family dependent upon him, whom he can neither educate nor provide for, thus being placed in a situation most distressing to a clergyman who for many years has faithfully served his country.

IX. That your petitioner refers his distressing case to the honour and justice of your honourable House, humbly begging your honourable House to grant him a committee to inquire into his case, and to award him reparation suitable to his sufferings.

And your petitioner as in duty bound will ever pray.

J. K. WALPOLE,
Late chaplain in Her Majesty's convict service.
Horndean, Hants, July 5th, 1858.

Appendix.

A true extract from Colonel Jebb's letter of December 12th, 1856, to the Rev. J. K. Walpole, informing him of his dismissal, and assigning the reasons for it:

45 Parliament-street, 12th December, 1856.
Sir,—　　　　*　　　　*　　　　*　　　　*

I have now to inform you, that having consulted my colleagues, we are unanimously of opinion, that it is a duty to look to the public interests, and that they cannot fail to be prejudiced by the continuance of any one in the execution of the important duties of chaplain, who has GIVEN THE SUPERIOR OFFICERS OF THE SHIP SO MANY AND SUCH JUST CAUSES OF OFFENCE. We are THEREFORE of opinion, that it will be most for the interest of the service, to make temporary provision for the discharge of those duties, and to release you from further attendance and responsibility.

*　　　　*　　　　*　　　　*　　　　*

I am, Sir, your obedient Servant,
The Rev. J. K. Walpole.　　　　(Signed)　　　　J. JEBB.

The following correspondence is remarkable as containing a public reply from Sir J. Jebb, who is entitled to all the benefit that reply can give him in the estimation of those who read the correspondence. The answer to Sir Joshua, signed "One who Knows the Truth," is by the Author, and never yet has met with a reply from Sir Joshua :—

CONVICT HULKS.—CASE OF REV. J. K. WALPOLE, IN THE "PHILANTHROPIST."

We have received the following document from the above-named gentleman, and we beg distinctly to state that we do not hold ourselves answerable for the truth of the assertions made therein. Mr. Walpole, however, assures us that there is nothing in the "statement" but what is true, and which he desires above all things to have an opportunity of substantiating in a public, free, full, and fair inquiry. Clearly, there is a very important principle involved in the case as represented by Mr. Walpole, and it vitally concerns every person in the Civil Service, that he should be able fearlessly, and without subjecting himself to unjust oppression, to bring before the proper authorities cases of abuse which may come within his knowledge, whether his complaint be of those above him or under him. We would by no means encourage frivolous complaints, but we think that affirmations made gravely and deliberately should be inquired into. Mr. Walpole says, "I could not be in the midst of so iniquitous an establishment as the hulks, and not make the attempt at least to draw Sir George Grey's personal notice to the state of things ; which, however, has only caused my own ruin, and not remedied matters. I could not receive in my ears the constant cries and groans of the wretched convicts, and hear Thomas Jones, who murdered Assistant-Surgeon Hope, Feb. 8, 1856, declare that they were at that pitch of desperation, that one object of his crime was, if possible, to draw public attention to the abuses of the place, without an effort to make such known where they ought to be known and remedied." Mr. Walpole gives it as his opinion, in which we are somewhat disposed to concur, that in reference to the appointment of governors, &c., over convicts, "the present military system and that supplied by only one small section of the army, a cluster of friends among themselves, in fact, instead of inviting the best men by open competition, will never produce the desired result, that of reforming convicts morally and spiritually, and duly preparing them for their eventual liberty." There is unquestionably at first sight an apparent judiciousness in selecting gentlemen accustomed by experience to a state of firm and steady discipline ; and if possessed of other necessary qualifications, military men might be the best adapted for such posts— but there is something more than mere disciplinarian capabilities required for the proper management of convicts ; and sure we are that many others exist who are far more fitted for the task than most military men, however eminent in their own special sphere. We know well that in a prison not many miles from London, a very large establishment is very efficiently and ably directed by a gentleman of the legal profession. The statement which Mr. Walpole has printed, and which has been forwarded to us, is as follows, and if it can be borne out, certainly appears to us to warrant him in expecting redress, at least in reinstatement to Her Majesty's service. We repeat, however, that we cannot answer for its truth, though it is not likely that

E

Mr. Walpole would have printed and circulated it as he has done had he not good grounds for his assertion.

The statement immediately preceding was then published. (See pp. 42-47,)

To that statement printed in the "Philanthropist" Sir J. Jebb sent the following answer :—

CASE OF REV J. K. WALPOLE.

To the Editor of " The Philanthropist."

45 Parliament Street, 24th Sept., 1858.

Sir,—My attention has been directed to a statement of the case of the Rev. J. K. Walpole, which appeared in your last number.

I would willingly have left Mr. Walpole in possession of any advantage he may have proposed to himself in printing and circulating through your pages such a statement, but as he only tells a part of the truth the impression he conveys is, as you suspect, very far from being correct.

The main object Mr. Walpole appears to have in view is to persuade his friends that he was illegally removed from the convict service by the Directors of Prisons, that the motives which actuated them, and myself in particular, were connected with personal private resentment, &c.

Now at the time Mr. Walpole penned the statement which appeared in your columns, he had in his possession a letter from the Under Secretary of State, dated 11th Dec., 1856 (the day preceding his removal), in which he was informed that Sir G. Grey, having referred to Mr. Walpole's letters to him of the 2nd of Oct. and the 6th of Dec., had been reluctantly compelled to adopt the conclusion that his further continuance in the office of Assist. Chaplain was inconsistent with the interests of the public service, and that he had requested the Directors to make arrangements for transferring the duties to another person, consulting, as far as was compatible with their duty, the convenience of Mr. Walpole as to the precise time at which his employment should terminate.

The discretion of the Directors was, under the circumstances, limited to a very brief period, and gladly would they have availed themselves of an opportunity of submitting a proposition that he should be continued in his office until the spring, a period of between three or four months, but at the very time that this subject was under consideration, circumstances occurred which precluded all hope of allaying the discord that had prevailed for so long a time, and the Directors had no choice, consistently with their duty, than that of recommending that Mr. Walpole should cease to perform the clerical duties on board. He, however, received his salary in the first instance to the end of December, and subsequently Sir G. Grey was good enough, on my making an earnest appeal, to sanction an additional quarter's salary. As regards the extracts which Mr. Walpole has given from the letters I addressed to him, the following more copious extracts will better explain the circumstances.

Extract from a Letter addressed by Colonel Jebb to the Rev. J. K. Walpole, 12th of Dec., 1856.

"Sir,—I had written a reply to your letter of the 9th instant, which would have been forwarded to-day, but I have this morning received from Mr. Waddington the copy of a letter he has addressed to you, from which

I find that the arrangement I had proposed in your favour will not now be carried into effect.

"I shall not further advert to your letter, but address myself to that part of Mr. Waddington's communication, in which he requests that the Directors will, as far as is compatible with their duty, consult your convenience as to the precise time at which your employment in the convict service shall terminate.

"I have now to inform you, that having consulted my colleagues, we are unanimously of opinion that it is a duty to look to the public interests, and that they cannot fail to be prejudiced by the continuance of any one in the execution of the important duties of a chaplain, who has given the superior officers of the ship so many and such just causes of offence.

"We are, therefore, of opinion, that it will be most for the interests of the service to make temporary provision for the discharge of these duties, and to relieve you from further attendance and responsibility.—I am, &c."

Extract from a Letter addressed by Colonel Jebb to the Rev. J. K. Walpole, 22nd of Dec., 1856.

"Sir,—I have received your letter of the 20th instant this day, and regret to find that it differs but little, either in spirit or expression, from those which you have before written.

"As regards the charges you prefer, they have already been investigated or will be inquired into.

"With respect to your saying that I have advised Sir George Grey to turn you and your family into the world in the middle of winter, for 'offending the superior officers of the ship,' that may be the light in which you may choose to view and represent the circumstances, but I can only say, you are entirely in error on both points.

"The arrangement I had proposed was one which under the circumstances was highly favourable to you, and you are yourself alone to blame for being now deprived of the opportunity of accepting it.

"I am not insensible to the painful position in which you have placed yourself and family by the course you have pursued. I should have hoped that the experience of the last twelve months would, if you had no better grounds, have led you to see that it was neither a wise nor a Christian course.

"After your treatment of myself, I can have no personal communication with you ; but if you desire my opinion, I would confer with any friend in whose judgment you can rely.

"Under any circumstances I should advise your consulting such a friend before you commit yourself further.—I am, &c."

Having limited myself to saying thus much in explanation, I would add that Mr. Walpole has a large family on whom an accumulation of undeserved misfortune has been brought, and that I believe them to be well deserving in every way of the kind sympathy of your readers.—I am, sir, your obedient servant,   J. JEBB.

The Author's reply, &c. to Sir J. Jebb—

To the Editor of the " Philanthropist."

London, October 22nd, 1858.

Sir,—I have only this day seen the reply of Colonel Jebb to the state-

ment of the Rev. J. K. Walpole, which you published last month.   As a
third party, knowing all the particulars which led to the dismissal of Mr.
Walpole, and which Colonel Jebb from reasons most potent shrinks from
publishing, I humbly request that you will allow me to make public,
through your columns, what are the causes that led to the cruel dismissal
of the Rev. J. K. Walpole.   I shall found my statement upon my personal
knowledge and upon documents now to be seen at the office of Colonel
Jebb, and at the Home Office in Whitehall.

1st., then, the Rev. J. K. Walpole complained to Colonel Jebb that he
was compelled by him to fulfil all the duties of a chaplain in a convict
prison, while the style and salary of only an assistant-chaplain was given
him.   Frequent and rather important correspondence passed between the
two on this point, and Colonel Jebb, to silence the reverend gentleman on
the troublesome point, hinted at his dismissal some years before it took
place.   Will Colonel Jebb send you that correspondence?

2nd. The Rev. J. K. Walpole made disclosures before a Commission of
Inquiry held in the Stirling Castle Convict Hulk in 1857, which commission was ordered by Sir G. Grey—those disclosures reflected very severely
upon the management of Colonel Jebb, and brought home to him the
responsibility of having allowed one of Her Majesty's prisons to get into a
most frightful state of anarchy and demoralization so late as the year 1856.
Will Colonel Jebb publish those disclosures?

3rd. The Rev. J. K. Walpole wrote to Sir G. Grey in 1856, to beg him
to spare the life of convict Thomas Jones, who murdered Surgeon Hope
in the Stirling Castle Hulk, in February, 1856; the reverend gentleman's
plea for mercy was, that the state of the hulk had led Jones to murder
Mr. Hope, and therefore his life he thought ought to be spared.   Mr.
Walpole had a reply to that application from Colonel Jebb, attempting to
throw upon Mr. Walpole the responsibility for the state of the hulk in
which he was chaplain.   Mr. Walpole then replied, and by several letters
showed Sir G. Grey that the fearful state of that hulk could not be
charged upon him, but that the blame rested with Colonel Jebb and the
Directors of Convict Prisons.   Will Colonel Jebb send you that correspondence?

4th. The Rev. J. K. Walpole complained repeatedly of indignities
which the officers of the hulk heaped upon him—which indignities the
writer has often witnessed with indignation and shame.   The reverend
gentleman proved the truth of his complaints, as the Directors themselves
ordered the amendment of several.   Will Colonel Jebb publish the correspondence that took place between him and the dismissed one on this
point?

5th. The Rev. J. K. Walpole pointed out to Sir G. Grey how kindly
Colonel Jebb had treated certain officers then and now in the convict
service who had been proved guilty of extreme irregularities and most
immoral crimes, in contrast to the treatment he himself had received.
Will Colonel Jebb permit the public to see who was right in that correspondence?

Lastly. The Rev. J. K. Walpole was coolly asked by Colonel Jebb to
acquiesce in a prospective dismissal, he having committed no crime, nor
having been called upon to answer any charge.   The reverend gentleman,

as a man and a gentleman, refused to be a party to his own official death. Then came a fearful drunken riot in the prison in which Mr. Walpole was sleeping: he reported the same, and for so doing he was—as Colonel Jebb's own letter does not deny—discharged without a hearing. Such, briefly, are the facts which led to Mr. Walpole's most unjust, most cruel dismissal; but, Sir, while he was discharged, those whom Sir G. Grey dismissed upon the report of his commissions in 1856, Colonel Jebb has retained in the convict service, although proved guilty of repeated acts of drunkenness—some of embezzling their accounts, and one of deeds not falling far short of manslaughter. I call upon Colonel Jebb to deny the above facts—he has all the records in his own hands, and the writer can supply him with names and dates if his memory fails him.

The fact is, Mr. Walpole was dismissed for daring to complain of the treatment he received from Colonel Jebb, and he is now suffering'from the tyranny of a military despotism, which has reigned, and now reigns, in all our convict prisons. I am prepared to give the public other important facts connected with this most painful business, but await, before doing so, a further reply from Colonel Jebb. In conclusion, I will only say, that Sir G. Grey told a clergyman that Colonel Jebb urged him to the dismissal of Mr. Walpole, and Colonel Jebb told the same clergyman that Sir G. Grey forced him to the act!

I send you my card, and remain,
ONE WHO KNOWS THE TRUTH.

To the Editor of "The Philanthropist."

Sir,—As an impartial "Philanthropist," you have well maintained your name, for which I sincerely thank you, in bringing under public notice the frightfully *excessive* and unchristian punishment which has been inflicted on me, through my dismissal, December 12, 1856, for having, as the chaplain, "offended the superior officers" of the "Defence" Convict Hulk, at Woolwich; and which punishment, now prolonged to close upon 700 agonising days and nights, it appears is to have no end. Having given the best years of my life to convicts, I had formed no connections beyond the convict employ, and thus now can neither support nor *educate* my family, I have no prospects upon earth. The Lord alone preserves my reason.

I am glad to see that Colonel Jebb, in his letter to you in this month's "PHILANTHROPIST," very fairly allows that my "Statement," which you published in your September number, contains the truth: he contradicts nothing in it.

But he should not have inconsistently written to you, farther on, speaking of me thus :—"The impression he conveys is, as you suspect, very far from being correct."

You never, Sir, in your remarks of September 4, used the word "suspect," nor any word akin to it in meaning: your sentiments seemed to be quite contrary. What *suspicion* of incorrectness did you intimate in these your introductory words ?—"We have received the following document from the above-named gentleman, and we beg distinctly to state that we do not hold ourselves answerable for the truth of the assertions made therein." You spoke here only as every *impartial* Editor would speak. I do not think there is such a man living as a *suspicious* Editor. Again, in your concluding words :—" We repeat, however, that we cannot answer for its truth, though it is not likely that Mr. Walpole would have printed and circulated it as he has done, had he not good grounds for his assertion." You intimate no *suspicion* here, Sir, that my statements are incorrect—rather the opposite; and Colonel Jebb himself allows that they are true, being, according to him, whatever their dimensions, " a part of the truth," to which he professes to add what is wanting. But let your readers judge, Sir, whether Colonel Jebb has added to my truth anything of value to throw light on the *mysteriousness* of this case of mine. He has passed by in silence my grave charges concerning Captain Gambier's secret inquiry at Woolwich, and the secret conference in London, in which Colonel Jebb, Captain O'Brien, and Captain Gambier, decided on my dismissal; in all which proceedings not the slightest chance was offered to me of escaping my doom before it was sealed.

It is a *well-known fact* that Colonel Jebb bore towards me a private ill feeling of *long standing;* and it was also in common circulation that there was an Assistant Chaplain to be provided for, who had been disappointed of the chaplaincy of a new Convict Prison, and that to my post that gentleman has been promoted, to upwards of £350 a year.

When Colonel Jebb speaks of " the discord that had prevailed for so long a time," he does not mention that Captain Warren, the Governor, was upheld in affronting and injuring me as he chose. He preferred against me a false charge in writing, that I had seriously neglected my duties on first coming to Woolwich, and which has been made, of course, to count against me, while to this day the Directors of Prisons have made no inquiry into it. By this and other wilful insults and aggressions made upon me, I would ask whether concord could be promoted, though, I solemnly assure you, the breach of becoming intercourse never arose on my side, nor did I show anything by words or demeanour to the offending parties. For the sake of peace, I acted too tame a part ; and thus, perhaps, invited the assault which has consigned me and mine to temporal destruction.

When Colonel Jebb speaks of a certain amount of salary paid to me after my dismissal, he cannot take credit to himself for this, for it speaks in my favour; and he can never mean that money can compensate for the dishonour and mental anguish and destruction of character which I have suffered at his hands.

As regards the reference made by Colonel Jebb to Sir George Grey, I now solemnly assure Sir George that he does not, to this day, know the truth, or he never *could* have sanctioned my dismissal for " offending the superior officers " of the Hulk—an offence of which I was not guilty, into which there has *never yet* been any inquiry in my presence, and which vague charge I assert to be ridiculously untrue and incapable of proof. The contrary I can satisfactorily prove.

As to the two letters from which Colonel Jebb has given extracts, I wish he had given them in full. On what there is I have no particular observation to offer, except that I remember remarking when I received them, that I could see, with reference to passing events, that they were written with a view to the possibility of future publication.

Private ill feeling not only caused my dismissal, but, it will scarcely

be credited, has pursued me since, of which the following is a specimen:—Eight months after my dismissal, when I was about to receive
an appointment abroad, I was suddenly cut off from it, the secret source
of which I know from proofs in my possession; while, at the same
time, every effort was made to induce me and my family to embark for
the place above referred to with an entirely free passage. Providence
alone frustrated what would have been to us so irrevocable a step.

Private ill feeling *still* pursues me to my injury under the calumnies
of "violent temper," and "always interfering in matters with which I
have no concern." I am said to be "of so violent a temper that none
of the convict officers could exist with me." This vague charge is
ridiculously untrue and incapable of proof, still one intance at least I
know in which it has injured me. Colonel Jebb has uttered with his
own lips to many that my "violent temper at Dartmoor kept the
prison in confusion." Captain Gambier was Governor of Dartmoor
Prison while I was there, and he and hundreds besides know that my
voice was never heard there above the common tones of duty, but all
know well who it was that did keep the prison in a ring through
violence of temper. Captain Gambier sees Colonel Jebb daily, and
nothing could have been easier or more Christianlike than to have
summarily stopped this calumny, but it appears he did not.

With regard to my "always interfering," &c., I can give a fair
sample of what has been called by this name. There was a convict,
J—— E——, who was about to receive a ticket-of-leave, but two years
before the usual time of it being due to him. On observing in the
books, connected with his name, "Known to the police of S—— for
twelve years as a bully to prostitutes," I thought such a character
must have been overlooked by the authorities in London, and therefore
wrote to them, pointing it out as a ground on which they might
perhaps defer the man's liberation, he having been in prison, I believe,
two years,—but I was answered that, as his ticket-of-leave was already
issued by the Home Office, it could not be interfered with. I have
known tickets-of-leave stopped the minute before a prisoner was about
to leave the prison. J—— E—— went to his liberty, and before long
rejoined his old companions, male and female, and, after being concerned in several ingenious and extensive burglaries, was taken, tried
at C—— Assizes, and received a fresh heavy sentence. This I read in
the newspapers, and have since received accounts from the mayor of
the borough, and the governor of the gaol. Such is a specimen of the
"interference," which, conceived in the best intentions, and conducted
in the most respectful manner, helped to treasure up against me
private prejudices and ill feelings, which caused my ruin. Still, I
believe that in such an instance as the preceding I was but discharging
my duty, and in neglecting to do what I did, I should have been
culpable. I discovered the other day that this calumny of "always
interfering," &c., is current in a certain high quarter, where, under
different circumstances, I might look for some substantial patronage.

I have to complain that, without my permission, Colonel Jebb has
taken the liberty to recommend my family to public charity, in the
conclusion of his letter to you, thus adding insult to injury. He speaks
of their "misfortunes" as "undeserved," and I must say that no one

knows better than Colonel Jebb that they are undeserved. There lived a man once, his name was Zaccheus, and of him we read, St. Luke xix. 8: "Zaccheus stood, and said unto the Lord; Behold, Lord, the half of my goods I give to the poor; and if I have taken anything from any man by false accusation, I restore him fourfold." This was a plain honest man, who acted up to what he professed. I have made no appeal myself to public charity, nor do I intend to make it; but I do ask all my Christian friends for their best prayers on our behalf, and their aid and co-operation in getting my case so brought forward into public, that I may obtain from the Home Secretary a fair, free, full, and public investigation into my wrongs. Very heavy damages are due to the *mode* of my dismissal, *illegal*, because brought about by a secret *conspiracy*, and for the injuries my character has received, so as to prevent me supporting and educating my large family.

I am, Sir, your obedient Servant,

J. K. WALPOLE,

Late Chaplain in Her Majesty's Convict Service.

Plumstead, Kent, October 25, 1858.

Editor's remarks in the same number of *The Philanthropist* :—

CONVICT HULKS.—CASE OF REV. J. K WALPOLE.

Our readers will be pleased to remember, that we have distinctly repudiated any private knowledge or personal bias in this matter. We are simply desirous that neither the weak should be oppressed by the strong, nor the weak vilify the strong with impunity. As we before stated, there is an important principle involved in the case. It is an Englishman's glory that he may not be punished for fault or crime, without an opportunity given to him to answer the charges brought against him, with his accuser face to face. This in our eyes is the *gravamen* of the above case, which Colonel Jebb may be able to remove. If the statements made by Mr. Walpole, in reference to the Convict Hulks, be correct, they should be matter of inquiry elsewhere than in our pages; indeed, the public welfare is deeply involved in such an inquiry, and it would ill become us to do more than draw public attention : this we have ventured to do, and Colonel Jebb has sent his rejoinder, which appeared in our last number. This has drawn forth two letters, one from Mr. Walpole, and another from "*One who knows the Truth*," who indeed appears to have had good opportunity for doing so, who, from his position and occupation, we are bound to believe, would only write what he conscientiously felt to be true, and who candidly and freely consents to his name being given to Colonel Jebb, if required. To these two letters we feel compelled in fairness to give insertion, but we are by no means disposed to continue a correspondence which cannot possibly bring the matter to a conclusion. We can draw attention to the case, and this we have done. Colonel Jebb, if he pleases, is justly entitled to his answer; but there we must stop. We can hardly imagine that the right of an Englishman to a hearing before punishment, has been in this case outraged. If so, it were indeed a subject for grave consideration. Official power may unwittingly be exercised with severity ; we can imagine that underlings may be afraid to speak the truth, which may take away their bread from them; but we repeat our former statement, that it vitally concerns every person engaged in the Civil Service, that he should be able fearlessly, and without subjecting himself to oppression, to bring before the proper authorities cases of abuse which may come within his knowledge, whether his complaint be of those above or under him.

Sir Joshua Jebb declined to give any reply to my pointed letter, although that reply was anxiously asked for by Mr. Baker, a magistrate, in an ensuing number of the same journal. Another letter (subjoined) was printed, from Mr. Walpole.

To the Editor of the Philanthropist.

Sir,—I beg to offer you my hearty thanks for having inserted my letter of October 25th in your November number, and, while I would not attempt to encroach upon your columns, I would beseech you to give a place to this letter in your next issue for December. It is true I have found by sad experience that letter-writing will never settle this painful business of mine ; still, Sir, by your aid in granting me this additional favour, the matter may be brought into that channel that at last a fair public investigation shall become unavoidable.

I have before this stated over and over again that I court a public investigation : I now demand it. In this, I think, I shall have the support of all my brethren, the prison chaplains, indeed, of all members of her Majesty's civil service. To every one of them I could say, as Horace said, after giving the anecdote of his Athenian miser—" Mutato nomine, de te," &c.

The following copy of a note, which I have recently received, will show the position to which I am reduced, as a subject of the Queen, in her world-wide empire, where the sound of Christ's blessed Gospel is never unheard as the revolving sun carries round the rolling hours of each day. You shall know by it, and by what I shall besides tell you, that my punishment is carried to the bounds of endurance—that my "name is cast out as evil,"—that, in fact, I am cast out with those with whom " no man might buy or sell," &c. (Rev. xiii. 17.)

I have already given you to understand that, since my unrighteous dismissal, I have been pursued with the most unfounded calumnies, which have cut me off from the hopes of church livings, and even curacies.

The note to which I refer is from the patron of a living, who, from the great age of the incumbent, was looking out for a curate. It is as follows:
"C——, Nov. 9th, 1858.

" Rev. Sir,—Under the circumstances of your case, I much regret that I am about to disappoint you ; but I feel so sure that —— (the rector) would agree with me in considering you ineligible for the curacy, that I have no other course to take.—I am, &c., ——."

You may suppose, Sir, that this was a heavy blow to me, as I had looked forward to this curacy as *a haven for the winter*. Now I know not what step to take, nor whither to turn. It is only He who is "touched with the feeling of our infirmities, and was in all points tempted like as we are," who can guide me, and dispose the hearts of His followers to look into my wrongs. After being in holy orders close upon a quarter of a century, and now turned adrift upon the world, with every avenue closed against me, through the calumnies which are sown broadcast, as I have found, through England, I think you, and every dispassionate judge, will decide that I have been punished with a vengeance for having "offended the superior officers" of the convict hulk *Defence*, at Woolwich. It is above twenty-one years since I commenced my first duties with her Majesty's convicts, and I challenge all the governors and officers that I have worked with, anywhere in the world, to come forward, and state *upon oath*, that my conduct was not *invariably* that of a gentleman. All the schoolmasters and Scripture-readers of prisons with whom I have worked would affirm what I state ; and I know that the hundreds upon hundreds of convicts with whom I have had dealings would say the same. I feel sure, Sir, therefore, you will give me all the aid in your power towards clearing my name from the cruel dishonour and falsehood which has been cast upon it.

I beg, Sir, you will allow me to add to the remarks which, by your favour, I have already made public, on Colonel Jebb's letter in your October number, that Colonel Jebb in that letter does but give a farther description than I had done of the weapons by which I was destroyed, although he professed to inform you of the truth. I would remind Colonel Jebb that the *roots* of the *real truth* date much farther back than the two or three letters to which he made allusion merely by their dates. He did not tell you that when, feeling my heavy responsibilities to my God, my queen, and my fellow-countrymen, I made a certain communication to Sir George Grey (March 20, 1856), he took offence at that communication, and wrote to me in such a strain that I saw his object was to pick a quarrel with me, and mark me, the chaplain, as the scapegoat for the amazing sins and iniquities of the convict establishment. I would only ask Colonel Jebb whether I did not tell him in my answer that I saw he intended me for the "scapegoat," and whether in about eight months thereafter he did not bring his designs to pass.

I advance nothing, nor ever have, nor will, but what I can prove in public ; and then the public will see how their interests have been sacrificed. But how, Sir, *can* the public know anything of these matters until some one devoted to destruction through them shall bring them to the light ?

The public know absolutely nothing, nor can know, nor ever will, concerning our dark, secret, and mysterious prison system, until they demand an open explanation. It may be all very well for a time for a wealthy and luxurious community to content themselves with "*fiant experimenta in corporibus vilibus;*" but——I will say no more.

The whole of the correspondence which I have carried on will be published in due time.

I must beg your permission to remark that, when Colonel Jebb says my dismissal was the only remedy remaining to allay the "discord" which prevailed, he could not have remembered how differently he treated my predecessor. He was charged with the same alleged offence as myself, and by all accounts "discord" raged ; still the above-named gentleman was only *removed* elsewhere by Colonel Jebb, and he is chaplain of a convict prison to this day.

I perceive that "One who Knows the Truth" has addressed you, and of this I knew nothing until, meeting him, he told me he had written to you. His letter speaks for itself, and requires no comment from me, except just to say that I should hope Colonel Jebb will candidly and straightforwardly reply to *all* his heads seriatim. Sir G. Grey's Commissioners, to whom he alludes, were Messrs. Perry and Arnott,—in February, 1856; and I would most respectfully call upon the Right Hon. the Home Secretary, as he values the Queen's honour and his own, to publish the evidence taken by Messrs. Perry and Arnott, and their Report to the Home Secretary; also, the evidence taken by Captain O'Brien, Captain Whitty, and Captain Gambier, in April, 1856 (just previous to the Governor's absconding), with their Report. And lastly, the evidence given before Mr. Hall, of Bowstreet, in November, 1857, with his Report.

You may believe me, Sir, when I assure you that your correspondent, "One who Knows the Truth," is *a man of truth*, and is so known and respected by his circle of friends, some of them in high positions.

I call upon you to witness, Sir, whether you cannot perceive, by my letters, that I am most anxiously desirous for a *public* investigation; while, on the contrary, what you have seen in reply evidently deprecates any farther publicity.

By inserting the above, as an impartial and Christian "philanthropist," you will deeply oblige,

Sir, your faithful servant,

J. K. WALPOLE,

Late Chaplain in Her Majesty's Convict Service.

Plumstead, Kent, November 24, 1858.

Mr. Walpole has publicly made his charges, without refutation or denial on the part of those against whom they have been made; the following notice of a lecture by that gentleman is a remarkable proof that he does not shrink from the consequence of any of his charges :—

In accordance with the wishes of his friends in Gosport, and elsewhere, the Rev. J. K. Walpole, late Chaplain of Her Majesty's Convict Invalid Establishment (formerly at Gosport), will state a series of facts from the following sources, and connected with his dismissal from H. M. Service, at the Crown Assembly Room, Gosport, on Friday, June 25th, 1858.

"And to shew thy pity upon all prisoners and captives."—*Litany.*

"We have little doubt that under our present prison system, such restraints as this "body belt" are occasionally necessary, because, if we make brutes, we must manage them when we have made them; still the question remains whether we need make men brutes. * * * * Would these men be such desperate wretches if they were not subjected to our modern refinements of punishment."—*Times*, December 18th, 1857.—Editorial article on the trial of Convict Joseph Weaver, at Exeter.

UNPUBLISHED FACTS CONNECTED WITH OUR HOME AND COLONIAL CONVICT SOCIAL EVIL.

I. The *Stirling Castle*, invalid hulk, Gosport—unfitness of the officials

—harsh and unjust treatment of the convicts; their consequent insubordination and ferocity—causes which led to the murder of the lamented Surgeon Hope, which was followed by the soothing of the convicts—Messrs. Perry and Arnott's inquiry by Sir George Grey's order—the governor both *absconds* and *resigns*, for which see police gazette, June 6th, 1856, and convict blue book for 1856—new governor and deputy. governor—Incessant punishments and aggravation of the evils—more attempts at murder—first removal of the establishment to Woolwich.

II. The *Defence* hulk, Woolwich. Things not amended by the change —Rev. J. K. Walpole, chaplain, dismissed without a hearing, because he had "given so many and such just causes of offence to the superior officers," (see Colonel Jebb's letter of December 12th, 1856.)—description of a drunken orgy in the *Defence* of a most outrageous nature, by the deputy governor and steward, superior officers—the *Defence* burnt—report to the Home Office that spontaneous ignition of the coals was the cause of the conflagration—convict known who set the hulk on fire—second removal of the establishment to Lewes.

III. Lewes prison, Sussex. State of affairs still worse—serious rebellion in September, 1857; its causes—medical officer nearly murdered by convict Stanley; his life saved by warder Strugnell—rebellion quelled by temporary chaplain and schoolmasters, and followed by the authorities granting the demands of the convicts—inquiry at Lewes prison by Sir. George Grey's order, in November 1857—Necessary conclusions from the preceding

IV. The Bishop of Perth (Western Australia). His opinion (in pamphlet on transportation) on the unfitness of convict officials—his letter (*Daily News*, March 18th, 1858,) on the frightful rebellion in the *Nile* convict ship—his apprehension of a horrible catastrophe in Western Australia—his words concerning the home convict authorities—great social peril incurred by us all—a subject for prayer.

Notice will be taken of the excessive punishment, and undeserved ruin, inflicted on the Rev. J. K. Walpole, and the unfounded calumnies which have been circulated to his detriment—various particulars—conclusion.

Notice of the Lecture in the local paper:—

On Friday se'nnight the Rev. J. K. Walpole (formerly of Gosport), late chaplain of her Majesty's convict establishment, stated "A Series of Facts," at the Crown Assembly Rooms, North Street, in illustration of the mismanagement of our convict establishments, and the dreadful results attendant thereon. The lecture consisted of statements to show that improper persons were in authority, and that, as a consequence, the prisoners had been in a state of revolt, and the murder was committed of a very worthy medical officer. Mr. Walpole made representations to the governor at the head of the department in furtherance of his opinions, especially of what he called a drunken orgie, continued through a Saturday night until Sunday morning. An inquiry was made into this representation, and the result was not that the officers accused were reprimanded or discharged, but that Mr. Walpole was dismissed for being, as alleged, troublesome to the officers. At the lecture Mr. Walpole as-. serted the truth of the accusation, having himself heard the noise and revelling. A gentleman from the convict establishment, however, denied it, and averred that it was only a convivial meeting! Mr. Walpole has been nearly twenty years connected, as chaplain, with the establishment. A Mr. Thwaites, recently schoolmaster in the establishment, has also been discharged, after nearly completing twenty years' service, for alleged troublesome interference. It is not stated against him that he has neglected his duty, or done any criminal act. It does not, perhaps, occur to the governor that these discharged men have actually forfeited a retiring pension, of which they are deprived by dismissal, but so it is: and taking Mr. Walpole's statements as indisputable, it appears to us that an undue amount of severity has been carried out in this hasty dismissal. A desire to see the jurisprudence for our convict establishments properly administered appears to have been the leading reasons which prompted the communication to the authorities. Colonel Jebb, however, viewed it in another light, and the dismissal of Mr. Walpole was accompanied with a notice that he was dicharged because he had "given so many and such just causes for offence to the superior officers." The lecture was well attended, and was listened to with deep interest, the dreadful murder on board the *Briton* being still fresh in the memory of most of those present.

Such, gentlemen, in brief, are some of the facts that will be brought before any rightly constituted public inquiry, to show that Sir J. Jebb is deluding the country, and has long been permitted, under the assumed garb of a convict prison reformer, to engraft upon the hulk system a system which is producing in its effects, both upon officers and convicts, fruits far more painful and demoralising than were ever known when the miserable convicts were confined in the dreadful hulks. The following article from the *Press*, January 2, 1858, will give in few words a true picture of the system:—

It is high time that a little daylight should be let in upon our convict system. The atmosphere with which Colonel Jebb has been permitted to invest that system, is so murky, as to be impenetrable to the eye of the public. In fact, it is only by occasional explosions that we are reminded that we are standing on a mine of Jebbism—for Colonel Jebb *is* the convict prison system just as Mr. Rowland Hill *is* the Post-office, as Sir C. Trevelyan *is* the Treasury, and Mr. Chadwick *was* the New Poor Law. Sir. G. Grey, as Home Secretary, is legally responsible for the doings of Colonel Jebb, and it is full time that Parliament should make Sir G. Grey understand that the responsibility he incurs is most serious. But we will not do Sir George the injustice to suppose that he really exercises an independent and proper authority in the matters concerning convicts. It is impossible that, as a man of humanity and justice, he can deliberately approve of all that is done in his name: he simply endorses and gives legal authority to the decrees of others.

The system pursued in our convict prisons may be easily described as in fact and reality an irresponsible despotism. No one can get at the real "secrets of the prison-house." Colonel Jebb, indeed, presents annually to Parliament a "Report of Convict Prisons," which just tells Parliament as much as, and no more than, Colonel Jebb chooses to tell—which is, in general, as near nothing of all that it would be desirable to know as may be. Sometimes he travels out of his road to panegyrise a pet officer, or to notice one who has incurred his displeasure ; and we shall call public attention to one or two of his exploits in this way to be found in his "Report" for 1856, which, by-the-way, was not presented to Parliament until August, 1857. But, in general, Jebbism consists in absolute dark-· ness, and a sort of Oriental seclusion. There is the Rock of Portland, with its twelve or fourteen hundreds of convicts. No man not an official or a prisoner can get inside that gloomy dungeon—you might as well attempt to scale the heights of Gibraltar. No lady, except the wives of Sir G. Grey and Mr. Gladstone, was ever known to penetrate that rock. It is indeed a virgin fortress. Dartmoor is equally mysterious—buried in soli- tude and desolation. The government of these curious places is purely military—*why*, we don't know. Such a system in the midst of popular and free institutions is a strange anomaly, and such an anomaly as requires either to be justified or given up.

There are three autocratic directors of convict prisons—three criminal triumvirs—Colonel Jebb, Captain Gambier, and Captain O'Brien. The governors of convict prisons are, of course, military men. What on earth there is in the education, habits, or experience of a smart martinet in the army or navy, to fit him for the office of governing convicts—an office requiring for its proper discharge a singular combination of high qualities —we have not the remotest means of conjecturing ; but such is Jebbism.

To come, however, to one or two cases in point of the irresponsibility of the present system. The Governor of Lewes convict prison is a Captain Warren, a young man who has smelt powder in India, both in the cavalry and infantry. He has, therefore, a *double* claim on Colonel Jebb's admira- tion. The Deputy-Governor of that favoured prison is a Mr. Finnie. The Deputy-Governor dwells in the prison, whereas the Governor comes in only at certain times. The Deputy is the person on whom the management of the convicts depends quite as much as perhaps, even more than, on the Governor. Mr. Finnie was lately a Woolwich bombardier ! These are the two principal officers of the convict prison at Lewes, where an "inquiry" has just taken place. This was instituted by the senior schoolmaster of the gaol, named Thwaites. That gentleman thought he had reasonable ground of complaint against the Governor, Captain Warren, and complained accordingly. An "inquiry" took place. Of course, Colonel Jebb, Captain Gambier, and Captain O'Brien, together with an independent multitude of subordinates in the prison, all under the control and fear of Captain Warren, came to the rescue of that imperilled warrior. Mr. Thwaites was voted calumnious, and Sir G. Grey has just *dismissed* him— a severe and cruel step, only to be justified by excessive ill-conduct. But such is the military system !

Mr. Thwaites is the second civil officer who has been dismissed by Colonel Jebb within the last twelve months. In December, 1856, Colonel Jebb dismissed the Rev. J. K. Walpole from the Chaplaincy of the *Defence*, convict ship, on the ground that "he had given just and repeated offence to the superior officers of the ship." Captain Warren was the governor of the *Defence*, and Mr. Finnie the deputy. The *Defence* was set fire to in June last, and the prisoners, being smoked out, were sent partly to Millbank Prison and partly to the *Unité* convict ship at Woolwich, from which ship Captain Warren and his cargo of convicts were removed to Lewes in September last. Mr. Walpole has acted as chaplain to criminals for twenty years. He is a man of excellent character; yet he was dismissed by Colonel Jebb—deprived of his bread by that humane gentleman —for "having given offence to the superior officers of the ship."

His offence was as follows:—He had felt it his duty to "report" Captain Warren for taking the convicts out boating on Sunday, when they ought to have been attending the service of the church. He also "reported" Mr. Finnie, for that he, the said Mr. Finnie, being in command of the *Defence*, did on a certain Saturday night in September, 1856, get exceedingly drunk in company with the steward of the same ship. The uproar created by these two Bacchanalians was such, according to Mr. Walpole's statement, that it woke him. From potations, according to Mr. Walpole, they proceeded to cantations, and it was some way on in the small hours of Sunday morning before the revelry of the commander and steward of the ship was quiet. The chaplain very properly "reported" this extraordinary specimen of convict government. The result of this second report, added to the enormity of his first, was that he was *dismissed!* —turned adrift with his wife and eight children to fare as he might—by Colonel Jebb.

Now, we make no doubt our readers will not believe this story. We admit it to be so improbable as to be almost incredible. Yet we believe it to be literally, absolutely true—capable of complete and unquestionable corroboration. But if it *be* true, may we not reasonably ask how much longer such a system of abominable injustice and tyranny is to be endured? If Parliament does not take this matter up, it will abdicate its function as guardian of the public liberties of England.

Such are only a few facts to prove the need there is that the convict service should be entirely revised, that it should receive the light of day and be thrown open, as all other departments are, to the management of those who have proved their ability and fitness for the office they seek. When I was in the convict service, I did my best to get the service reformed; my views were expressed in the following letter which the *Daily News* did me the honour to publish in 1856 :—

COMPETITIVE EXAMINATION FOR OFFICE IN CONVICT PRISONS.

To the Editor of the " Daily News."

Sir, — Your able articles at various times upon competitive examination for office in the civil service, have been highly calculated, if rightly considered, to benefit the best interests of the country.

But competition should not be limited to candidates for the humbler offices ; it should be demanded from those who aspire to the more lucrative posts. I find that in many of the departments of the public service, the clerks, and the clerks only, are called upon to compete before they are admitted into Government employ. One of the departments where such is the case, is that part of the civil service denominated the *convict service.* I find, Sir, that the only officers who have to compete for office in the convict service are the clerks. Now, Sir, if you will permit me, I will endeavour to show, that competition for such an office, though of some importance, is of very trifling moment when compared with other offices which have to be filled. A clerk in the convict service is pretty much a copying machine; it is true he may have to, as I believe he often does, find brains for the governor under whom he serves, by composing his letters and drawing up his annual reports; but these things are not his legitimate business; he ought to be only a copying machine in a governor's office, so that an acquaintance with the simple rules of arithmetic, writing a good hand, and spelling properly, comprise all the talent his legitimate duties require. But as I am informed, the clerks at present have to bring before their examiners far higher intellectual attainments, position, and talent than seem to be expected from those officers under whom they are placed. It may be thought that these attainments are needful to enable the clerk to discharge the more important duties of a prison which belong to the office of a governor, to which rank he may hope to be appointed. If any clerk enters the convict service with such an aspiration, he very soon finds that he entered under the influence of a delusion.

In the convict service, merit and service count for nothing in the disposal of the highest appointments. A military education is now thought to constitute the indispensable requisite in the candidate for the appointment of governor, deputy-governor, and chief warder in convict prisons. Now, Sir, no one could complain of this, if competition gained for military men this distinction. But we find, whenever a vacancy occurs in a convict prison, either in the office of governor or deputy-governor, that a lieutenant, a captain, or a major receives the appointment. And it is very soon found that having been in the army was the only qualification he brought for the post. Now, Sir, as convicts and their reformation are becoming a great social question, it is of the last importance that they should be managed while in prison by men who can bring the utmost fitness to the work.

I propose, then, that governors, deputy-governors, chief warders, chaplains, schoolmasters, and religious instructors, should all pass through a proper examination to show their fitness, before being appointed to fill either of the above offices in the convict prisons.

Can we, Sir, expect reformation while we entrust the management of criminals to men who know nothing of the peculiar class whom they called upon to govern? I believe it is a notorious fact, that the great majority of those men who have been governors and deputy-governors of convicts under the present convict prison board, have done nothing in the way of the reformation of convicts. This is not surprising; they came to a work to which they brought no knowledge—a work quite foreign to their tastes; the only claims they had for the appointment being, that they had interest with Colonel Jebb and had been in the army.

I know a little, Sir, of prisons upon the continent, and they will bear a comparison with ours; in fact, we are required to blush, when comparing our success with the success of some—nay, many—of the continental prisons. I find that military governers of prisons on the continent are the exception, not the rule. Those who have brought about the best system of prison treatment—the most humane and at the same time the most reforming and deterring—have all been civilians.

Our convict prisons should be governed only by men who have first proved their competence in the following manner:—They should be required to write an original essay upon prison systems—proving their knowledge of the various methods, past and present, for the reformation of criminals. They should also afford proof that they are not unacquainted with all the details of prison management, and possessed likewise some knowledge of the causes of crime. They should be men who have led temperate lives, out of debt, and bring to the work a character for high morality, and I would not except piety. Deputy-governor and chief warder should do the same.

Chaplains are even more important in prisons than governors. They should pass a searching examination in all the points required from the governor. They should never be appointed chaplains until they had proved their fitness by passing through a prison as an assistant-chaplain. Their own reports should not be, as now, the testimonials to gain them an appointment.

Next in importance to chaplains in prisons rank the schoolmasters; they have daily intercourse with the convicts, and upon their teaching depends mainly the moral and intellectual improvement of criminals. Now I am aware that there are some men, schoolmasters among convicts, who are highly qualified for this work—but there are again many others who, if their attainments had been tested, would never have gained admittance even into a village school. The work of a convict schoolmaster is highly important. He should be a man of mind—a man holding sound moral and religious principles; he has to come into daily contact with some of the cleverest of his species, but, alas! with men who have too often prostituted the highest talents to the basest of purposes. Such men become disgusted when they find themselves put into a class in a prison school to listen to a man who cannot put together in a compact manner a simple English sentence; whose mind has never comprehended more than the simple rules of arithmetic, with reading and writing. A prison schoolmaster should be one, who in teaching from history, science, or Scripture, is able to prove the folly of acting upon wrong principles, and set before his class the advantage of doing well. Competition should be required before a schoolmaster should be received into the convict service, and when once in he should rise not by favour, but by his merit and service.

Religious instructors should also gain admittance only by proving their fitness for their work. Their office is to read and explain the word of God to the sick and dying, and though they do not require so high attainments, intellectually and literally, as schoolmasters, none ought to be allowed to fill such an office who are not devotedly pious.

Why should not a prison warder, a clerk, a schoolmaster, or a religious instructor, have the opportunity to rise to be governor, if he proved his fitness? Should not merit, and merit alone, be the qualification?

Every French soldier is said to carry a field-marshal's baton in his knapsack—but it is only commissioned officers in the army that at present can hope to gain the office of a convict prison governor.

I, therefore, as a citizen of this proud England, enter my protest against such an injustice—such a miserable folly; and as convicts are becoming a terrible fact in our social system, I call upon the country to turn their attention to the matter, and, as in other departments, so in this, demand that the right man should be put in the right place, and that a military clique should no longer have the sole control of English convicts.

Liberated convicts are fast multiplying in our streets, and it behoves us

F

to look well to it that our money voted for their management should be most wisely spent, and that one person should no longer have the selection of every convict officer—and such selection be guided by no principle, but his own choice,

I am, &c.,   Civis.

Having shown in this letter that Sir G. Grey allowed Sir J. Jebb to throw me upon the world, with loss of pension, and as far as he could without a character, I will place before your lordships and gentlemen the character given me the day after my dismissal, by those who knew my efforts and had worked in the service with me.

Lewes Convict Prison, Dec. 21, 1857.

I have great pleasure in testifying to the excellent manner in which Mr. Thwaites has discharged his duty as schoolmaster in this establishment for many years. I have always esteemed him highly as an active, clever, and energetic teacher ; that he is the sort of man to have an influence for good over those whom he may be called upon to instruct.

WILLIAM LAKE.
Religious Instructor.

Cliffe, Lewes, Dec. 19, 1857.

My dear Mr. THWAITES,—Having heard this morning of the sad result* of the late investigation, I cannot, and ought not, forbear writing a few lines of condolence to you.

From my knowledge of several of the charges, I cannot reconcile in my own mind this fearful issue with truth and justice.

I feel the more from the fact that during the long time we have worked together, I have ever found you zealous and conscientious in the discharge of your important duties.

That you have striven hard in the service to reform and enlighten the unfortunate men, both by teaching and example, as before God, I believe as strongly as now I feel sad; and I know that perhaps without an exception the prisoners also feel this to be true.

I feel that in your dismissal the service has lost one of the most upright and conscientious it is possible to find left behind.

I trust and believe that out of this dark dispensation, God will work out greater blessings for you.

I know you have been the instrument of comforting the sorrowful, of aiding and supporting the weak, of instructing the ignorant, and (as I believe) leading some to a Saviour. I trust that wherever you go, and whatever you do, God's blessing will always attend you.

I remain, my dear friend, very sincerely yours,

Mr. W. Thwaites.   JOHN BEVIS.†

Testimonials from Chaplains in the service with whom I have laboured—

I have much pleasure in complying with Mr. Thwaites's request to give

---

* My dismissal without an hour's notice.

† Now Religious Instructor at Millbank Prison, then Schoolmaster at Lewes, one of my witnesses ; since punished by Colonel Jebb, for daring to speak to the truths of what he knew.

him a testimonial expressive of my sense of his character and efficiency as a master in the schools connected with the Woolwich convict establishment. Mr. Thwaites has been, since I became acquainted with him, uniformly diligent and attentive in the discharge of his duties, and has succeeded not less in conciliating the regards of the men by his kind and gentle demeanour. I have personally examined him on subjects which he professes to teach, on English and ancient history, arithmetic, geography, and grammar, and have found him quite competent to the discharge of his duties.

I further believe Mr. Thwaites to be one who lives under the influence of the Gospel of our Lord Jesus Christ.

STEWART HANNA, Chaplain.

Woolwich, March 1, 1849.

Shorncliff Barracks, August 21, 1851.

SIR,—I have much pleasure in bearing witness to the punctuality, diligence, and efficiency with which you have discharged your duties during the eight months you have been stationed as schoolmaster at this prison.

I am, yours truly,

Mr. Thwaites. RICHARD YERBURGH, Chaplain.

In conclusion, I will name to your lordships and gentlemen that many of the leading Members of both Houses of Parliament have expressed their desire to see the matter investigated. This not from one side of the House, but from both. But the writer is a poor man. He is humble; and, as yet, has found nothing but his own right hand and the Providence of God to help him. The following letter by Mr. Disraeli to a friend, a clergyman, when asked to bring the matter forward in the House of Commons, will suffice to show that it is not the Author's fault the matter has not come before the public :—

Grosvenor Gate, Dec. 15, 1857.

MY DEAR ——,—Your letters came to me when I was much pressed. I have not been able to consider them, and have so much on my hands that I see no prospect of doing justice to the subject.

I think that Mr. Henry Baillie would bring forward the matter very well. He is a clear and vigorous speaker, very industrious, and not to be influenced by petty or personal considerations. As an old Etonian, probably you know him; and, if you think proper to write to him, you can use my name. His certain address, "to be forwarded," would be at his father's, Mortimer Street, Cavendish Square.

Yours sincerely, D.

In the meanwhile, this friend had applied to Mr. Newdegate, who promised to bring the matter forward, but failed in his kind effort; as Sir G. Grey went out, and Mr. Walpole came in. The same friend, before this, had placed the matter before Mr. Walpole ; but, as soon as he became Home Secretary, when applied to, peremptorily refused to do anything to give either the Author or Mr. Walpole justice.

Thus, then, the Author has been driven to disclose facts of a most serious nature : thus has he been driven to open the eyes of Parliament to the condition of the convict service ; and upon these grounds it is, that he seeks a public court of inquiry—that the details which he has kept back may be publicly known, and a remedy applied to all the frightful abuses which have crept in, and been fostered, by the management of the convict service under Sir J. Jebb.

The Author has kept from publishing all the sickening details he has witnessed, and he hopes that he may never be driven to place upon permanent record the frightful horrors which he personally knows of the convict service of so-called Christian England.

To show that the Author is not the only person who has published the true character of Sir J. Jebb's system, I quote the following from a letter to Sir Joshua, published by Horsey, Portsea, written by Major Stewart, late Governor of Chatham Prison :—

After my removal from Chatham Prison I took the opportunity of reminding Captain Gambier "that had he not encouraged the Governor in his insults to me, I should still have retained office ;" and what think you was his sapient reply—" How could I help it ! ! !"

Could an enemy have given utterance to a more trite expression of this very grand and very portly gentleman's incompetency ?

Before I conclude this letter it is due I should allude to a remark or two which you made to me, and perhaps will make to others, by way of justifying yourself with respect to the line of conduct you have pursued—you reminded me that "there is no one in the convict service for whom you had done so much" as myself ! From what I have learnt from others, this is one of those phrases peculiarly your own, which you employ in assigning a reason for passing over the claims of an officer, or dispensing with his services.   But you also remarked that I had quarrelled with the Governor of Portland Prison ?   What grounds, Sir, had you for this assertion ?   Absolutely none whatever !   Your statement was a fabrication : indeed, when I denied it, you had to fall back to the remark, " *you* knew there was something."   No, Sir, I had no misunderstanding with the Governor of Portland Prison, or any other officer of the establishment.   That Governor is still in his office, and I defy him, with truth, to assert the contrary.   You must have been aware that I had had no quarrel with the Governor of that Prison ; and you must be also aware that I am not the only person you have maligned in this manner.   But it is quite consistent with yourself, when a man is dismissed, or passed over by the promotion of others, to remark, " He is quarrelsome, injudicious, indiscreet, troublesome, or has lost influence with the officers and prisoners "—very vague and general charges, which would not be worth notice did they not furnish you with a weapon wherewith to inflict wounds upon your unfortunate victims.

Although I have sustained this injury at your hands, I write not in anger, but to do myself justice with those before whom you have endeavoured to injure my reputation by removing me from my position at Chatham.

To me, who for many years held a commission in the army, it is truly lamentable to see one who holds her Majesty's commission so far forget that sense of honour, justice, and conscientious dealing, as your transactions with me have manifested.

From what I have seen and heard, however (and I have lately perused a statement of your cruel treatment of that unfortunate man, the Rev. Mr. Walpole, once a chaplain in the convict service), it seems only a part of a plan, which in a greater or less degree guides you in your official dealings with the department unfortunately placed under your direction; and in which you are influenced not by any real desire to promote the public good, but to serve those friends who have helped you to attain a status to which you could not otherwise have aspired.

How many officers in the Convict Department could I enumerate, who perform their duties in the most efficient and satisfactory manner, who are not promoted, because they lack noble friends, or have the misfortune to see that matters connected with the department are not in that perfect condition which your reports represent, or because they will not submit to be called "impertinent," or, when censured without cause, whether by yourself or a Visiting Director, have the boldness to complain of the injustice. Your prison system, Sir, whether "silent" or "public works" system, is a sham. I will leave others to say in what terms the manner in which you perform your "public duties" shall be described—believing, however, that it cannot last, and that the days of your power, which you have so much abused, are nearly run.

Trusting in the future, and that eventually justice will prevail, I remain, at present, one of your victims,

September, 1859.   H. W. S. STEWART.

C. P. Measor, Esq.'s published opinion of Sir Joshua's system and Palatial Prison :—

It is not a little strange that a system, which commences with uselessly stern separation, ends with the indiscriminate congregation of criminals; and this mistake seems to have reached its culminating point in the construction of the last "model" prison for public works at Chatham, where there are 1,104 small separate corrugated iron cells in one undivided building; the consequence being, that no half dozen prisoners can misconduct themselves, by making disorderly noises in their cells, but the example is communicated to the entire prison. The interior of this building has a pretty light effect, and is generally thought, particularly by the ladies who visit it, very much to resemble an aviary on a large scale; but all those who have practically tested its capabilities as a prison, must concur in the opinion that it is a great constructional mistake, multiplying the difficulties of management, and, on any occasion of general disaffection among the convicts, not unattended with positive danger.

The principles of discipline are as much involved in the ground-plan of a prison as in its management; and it is therefore much to be regretted that errors long ago made apparent are constantly being reproduced in new buildings, simply because practical men, and those who have to use them, are rarely, if ever, consulted. Convict Prison buildings have cost the country no less than £818,215 in the last twelve years, and it is consequently a matter of no small importance that their arrangements should be as complete and practical as possible. One point attended with much unnecessary public expense deserves special mention. Convicts who for misconduct are remitted to a second or third probation in separate confinement, have to be sent back from a Public Works prison to one of the metropolitan ones, because there are not sufficient cells in the Public Works prisons for carrying out the separate system. The consequence is, that many of them are induced to misconduct themselves merely to get a change of prison; in fact, would take a good deal of punishment for the pleasing variety of a journey by railway and through the streets in an omnibus.

I return for a moment, however, to the consideration of the present system of Convict reward, and must state, as the experience of many old officers, with whom I have conversed on the subject, that there is much less humility and respect evinced by the convicts under the present system than formerly, while these do not seem to have been replaced by any true or manly independence. It is rather the effrontery of assured insolence in the possession of rights, and the necessary result of attaching large rewards to bare and negative excellence; miscalling lazy work industry, and sufficient cunning to keep out of reports, good conduct. The true want in prison training is a plan for thoroughly and practically developing the character of each individual in good acts, which may acquire the force of habit, when he is left without the support of a system. Prisoners should be made to be respectful, orderly, cleanly, and obedient, irrespective of reward; and it is as absurd to attach a shilling a week to the fact of a convict's not assaulting his warder, or being insolent, as it would be to reward free men for keeping the Queen's peace toward their neighbours, or guarding their hands from entering other people's pockets. You thus destroy the first idea with which prisoners should be impressed, namely, that laws must be respected either for their own sake or from fear of punishment.

The following quotations show how Sir Joshua Jebb's Convict System prepares men for the Colonies :—

I must now allude briefly to one of the worst evils in the entire system, and one which calls for immediate remedy—I mean, the mode of Convict transportation. In consequence of the prisons of Bermuda, Gibraltar, and Western Australia, being under the charge of the Colonial Secretary, it may be possible that the Home Department has but little to do with it; but the responsibility to the public and to common morality must rest somewhere. The country has spent hundreds of thousands, if not millions, in carrying out the principle of separating prisoners at night, by giving them distinct sleeping-berths; and it is a wise and proper precaution, well worth whatever it may have cost. Yet, in sending large batches of the very worst criminals year by year from our shores, there are no means taken to maintain throughout voyages of months the least precautions against the abominable offences and contaminations which naturally result from their perfectly unrestricted association. Three hundred men are packed, "like a herd of condemned souls on their way to Tartarus," into the hold of a ship, with sleeping-berths in two rows, one above the other, giving a space of about sixteen inches by six feet to each prisoner. What becomes, may I ask, of all the previous discipline, moral teaching, and separate-confinement experience, on such a voyage? Is it not the greatest inconsistency, and the rankest folly, to delude oneself, that with men convicted over and over again—as these long-sentenced men have been—of every conceivable offence, the dictates of decency or morality will be followed; or to doubt that, freed from their previous restraint under such circumstances, they will become a mutual contamination to each other, and spend their time in recounting their criminal experiences, and gloating over the memory of their iniquities? Two years and a half ago I personally drew Sir Joshua Jebb's attention to this abominable system, when I was called from H.M.S. *Argus*, lying in Portland Harbour as an assistance in the suppression of the mutiny at that prison, to go on board the *True Briton*, awaiting orders to sail for Bermuda with convicts, among whom a mutiny was already threatened, and whom I found in a condition of rank insubordination. The issue of that voyage I will describe in the words of a corporal of artillery, who went out in the ship. He says:—

"It is only with God's help we got here. We had not been three months at sea, when the ruffians one night cut through the deck into the hold, and from that to the steward's room, and broke into that, and stole fifty pounds of tobacco and about twelve dozen of wine, brandy and rum, and also broke into the officer's baggage and stole all his jewellery. So after they had a good treat, and got well drunk, they proposed to work right up to where the soldiers were, and take us all by surprise; but they disagreed among themselves, and put it off for another day. A—— was to be captain of the ship, and take her to America. They even cast lots for the captain's wife, and all of us were to be killed but her."

The conduct of the prisoners who went out in the next ship, the *Sir John Lawrence*, to Bermuda, is described in the following language by one of the better-disposed convicts who was on board:—

"Could I sum up words, or foul my mouth with words, I might be able, perhaps, to give you a feeble idea of the doings that are carried on in a convict ship. It may be sufficient for me to say, I consider a convict ship a floating hell; and I thoroughly believe it was the mercy of God that prevented our going to our last account."

And yet, in spite of facts long ago brought to official notice, and in spite of the personal observation and report of the Bishop of Perth, upon this subject, the same scandalous system of transportation is continued, and no later than October last, the *Palmerston* sailed for Western Australia with over three hundred convicts huddled together in the same way as a festering cargo of human pollution. The system is so bad that a chaplain is never sent, whose presence, indeed, would merely be a solemn mockery; and it would really seem as if the only object were to get the most depraved class of criminals anywhere out of sight, regardless of the conditions of their existence, while we prate of the reformatory discipline of those who are left at home.* There are dozens of ships of war rotting in our harbours which could be repaired and fitted up with separate cells of thin corrugated iron, and converted to this special service; but what is

---

* No ignorance of the character of such prisoners can be pleaded, when special instructions are issued to select *those least fit to be set at liberty in this country.*

everybody's business is nobody's business, and so this monstrous abuse is permitted to continue a scandal to the country.* The propriety of sending convicts at all to our colonies who have done only a year out of sentences of from eight years to life, is more than questionable, as it is impossible abroad to secure an efficient staff of officers, or to maintain the discipline which can be kept up in the home establishments. The authorities out there being driven to make use of such means as are at hand, with prisons entirely on the associated system, as at Bermuda, laxity and immorality attain a luxuriant growth; and then from the prisons of Bermuda and Gibraltar, the convicts are sent back, after this training and the schooling of two such voyages, to contaminate for months our home prisons, and ultimately to be discharged, with large gratuities, as reformed. A glance at the record of the prison offences sent home with them is alone sufficient to condemn the system ; one of the most common being "drunkenness," sometimes even in chapel and school, for which the punishment usually assigned is the stoppage of their "grog." Their large earnings, often £20 and £30, constitute in some cases a sufficient inducement for them to abstain from prison outrages during the few months they are kept in the Public Works prisons; but the effect of such a punishment on their future life can easily be imagined. Western Australia, our only colony which will now consent to receive and retain our criminal refuse, will not long, I expect, be willing to do so, when the system of sending out men in the first stages of their sentences has borne its natural fruits ; but it might have been retained, and been exceedingly useful as a means of final disposal for men properly disciplined and tested to enjoy an earlier liberty on ticket-of-leave.

The failure of the present convict system—and that it is a failure seems placed beyond a doubt by the criminal statistics and the number of reconvictions—is to be attributed to the mode of its administration. Enough, and more than enough, of public money is expended upon it to make it an effective engine for crime suppression, and for returning into society men with, possibly, more trained intelligence and better principles than the ranks from which they come; but "the cup and platter" principle of discipline ceases with the prison walls, where men have spent years in the dull monotony of forced labour, without intellectual advancement, or plain instruction in their social interests and obligations. The hulks may justly have been denominated "Whited Sepulchres," † but the interests of the public have not profited much, if, with the erection of costly prisons, increased salaries, and enlarged prisoners' gratuities, they have merely secured "Pipe-clayed Sepulchres" in exchange for them. The combination of mere external discipline, and prison drill, with a religious teaching which encourages the affectation of spirituality, is about as unpractical a system of criminal reformation as could well be devised, and the whole intermediate ground between these two extremes requires judicious occupation. It is the prisoner's body which has sinned against the state, and

---

* A special staff of experienced officers could easily be selected, who would maintain discipline on the voyage, and, as far as possible, promote improvement and industry, instead of giving the convicts over to a surgeon-superintendent, and a lot of emigrant pensioners, who are totally unacquainted with their management, and probably never saw a convict before.

† See Sir Joshua Jebb's Report for 1856 and 1857, page 7.

as the punishment is inflicted upon that, it is from thence, in an ascending scale, that the work of reformation should be carried; but to leave the mind unenlightened, and the powers of thought unregulated, are the surest methods of perpetuating a distortion of the moral nature, and of implanting any higher principles upon no surer foundation than the imaginations and feelings.

Mr. Measor, for publishing the foregoing quotation (so it is alleged) has been dismissed from Chatham prison since the last outbreak:—

THE CONVICT PRISON AT CHATHAM.—Major Ogilvie, the new deputy-governor, has arrived at the prison and commenced his duties. The ground alleged for Mr. Measor's removal is having published a letter to Sir George Cornewall Lewis, on the administration, results, and expense of the present convict system. Yesterday morning another of the assistant-warders was discharged by an order from the Home Office. It is understood that an entirely new system of discipline will be introduced, and that the convicts will be required to be respectful, orderly, and obedient. There is to be a change of convicts, a certain class being sent to Portland, and another to Portsmouth and other prisons.—*Standard*, Feb. 21, 1861.

If Mr. Measor's statements are true the country has to thank him. That what I have quoted is true, I know from indisputable evidence, viz., my own senses, and those of other sane persons. Then Sir Joshua has added another victim to the number of his official slain. Mr. Measor has dared to let in murky light upon the horrors of the system; and, faint as that light is, it is thought worthy of an eternal extinguisher.

Since the outbreak at Chatham, eleven of the worthy and fit warders have been dismissed, and such confidence has the governor and Sir Joshua in the fitness of the remainder, that they have been told, they will be *instantly dismissed if they venture to speak of the late fearful riots in that well ordered prison.*

REIGN OF TERROR IN CHATHAM PRISON.

To the Editor of the Standard, Feb. 21, 1861.

SIR,—The officers in Chatham Prison are strictly prohibited from speaking to any one concerning the causes of the late bloody riots; if they mention the cause to their own family they are to be dismissed. Can the country allow such fearful terror as this to continue, simply that the truth should not be known?

Sir, a public inquiry would discover that the convicts had serious and just cause of complaint, and that it was the cruelty, tyranny, and misconduct of the chief officers that drove them into rebellion. Will Sir J. Jebb, Captain Gambier, and Captain Powell tell the public why it is needful to discharge Mr. Measor, the deputy governor. The public must have this matter investigated, and the officers at Chatham must not be turned out of the service if they speak the truth. I remain, &c., VERITY.

How very valuable must be the services of 100 officers, if a word or two upon a fearful outrage, spoken without the prison walls, can dismiss them.

OPINION OF THE PRESS ON MR. MEASOR'S LETTER TO SIR G. C. LEWIS, &c.

Nothing has yet transpired to show that the Government intend to institute such an open and searching investigation into the causes of the recent convict outbreak at Chatham as can alone satisfy the public mind. Sir Joshua Jebb and Captain Gambier are pursuing what they denominate an inquiry, but it is conducted with closed doors, and applications of brute force have been its only visible results. Men have been flogged wholesale by stout drummers till the prison yard has become a vast puddle of human blood. A hundred and five convicts have been chained together night and day, sleeping at night on boards in the wash-house and bath-rooms, and standing all day in the prison yard. The penitence displayed by these men, and their exemplary conduct during the week, induced the Governor of the prison, Captain Powell, to relieve them last Sunday from this degrading and senseless infliction. But Sir Joshua Jebb has annulled the merciful decree, and directed that twenty-three of the men should undergo a renewal of the same discipline until further orders. Between four and five hundred convicts are still in solitary confinement in their cells, upon a diet of bread and water, and are to remain in the same position for some time to come. All this is in obedience to the arbitrary edict of two official personages. The evidence upon which they have acted is carefully concealed; the manner in which they have conducted the inquiry is kept inaccessible to public criticism. Subordinate functionaries in the prison might probably tell strange tales if they dared. But their lips are sealed by the recollection that more than one of their colleagues has been dismissed for presuming to make unpleasant revelations. Fortunately, however, we have the evidence of one competent witness, who having resigned his appointment, has nothing to fear from the anger of his superiors. Mr. Measor, the late deputy-governor of Chatham prison, has addressed an admirable letter to the Home Secretary, which he has published in a pamphlet form; and though, having been written before the late revolt, it throws no direct light on the immediate cause which led to it, it yet indicates so forcibly some of the prominent defects of our existing penal system that it may be earnestly commended to general perusal.

The figures quoted by Mr. Measor show that if our convict system has failed to produce the salutary effects desired, it has not been from lack of expenditure. The cost of our home convict prisons has increased from 196,689*l.* in 1851, to 323,441*l.* in 1860; and although it is true that the partial cessation of transportation has had some share in creating this increased cost, it appears that between the periods named, the population of those prisons has only augmented from 6,390 to 8,286, so that the ratio of increase in expenditure has been one-third higher than that of the increase in numbers. The additional outlay appears to have been chiefly in the maintenance of the prisoners, the cost of which has increased at Portland 13*l.* 3s. 3d., at Portsmouth 11*l.* 12s. 2d., and at Chatham, as compared with the hulks for which it was substituted, 14*l.* 5s. 8d. per man per annum, during the interval between 1851 and 1860. Moreover, we have spent, during the last twelve years, 818,215*l.* in building convict prisons, so that it cannot reasonably be complained that there has been any stint of needful funds. Yet what is the result? Taking the first and last halves of the decade which has just expired, we find of the minor offences punished in gaols an annual average of 18,841 for the first five years, against 12,754 for the second; and of the graver crimes entailing death, transportation, or penal servitude, an annual average of 2,603 for the first five years, against 2,391 for the second. The criminals who have been punished in ordinary gaols have decreased 31·7, those who have undergone the discipline of convict prisons have decreased only 8·1 per cent. At the same time, the re-convictions of the latter class of offenders have largely increased; as an example of which Mr. Measor states that out of 1,400 prisoners who passed through Millbank Penitentiary last year, 300 confessed to former convictions, or could be positively identified as having been under previous sentences of transportation or penal servitude.

To what are we to ascribe this costly failure? Mr. Measor attributes it mainly to the two causes which we pointed out when treating of the subject a few days since—the influence of an imperfect system and the mismanagement of incompetent functionaries. The labour of the convict is productive of no advantage to himself, and, being thus devoid of natural stimulant, becomes ridiculously unproductive. In the construction of the new practice range in Plumstead and Erith Marshes in 1856, it was found that a navvy excavated eight cubic yards per day, a sapper five, and a convict two; and the result is, not only a serious loss to the State, but a total failure to cultivate those habits of industry, the want of which is a fertile source of crime. The gratuity system is absurdly framed; money rewards are bestowed for abstinence from actual misconduct, for length of prison service, and for the performance of labour as estimated by the officer placed in immediate charge of the prisoner, who receives an extra payment if he is believed to have stimulated the convicts to exertion, and consequently has a pecuniary interest in making a favourable report of their performances. The educational training of the criminal is too exclusively under the control of the chaplain, and, consequently, does not even professedly aim at the inculcation of those secular truths which will make him a better citizen when he is released from bondage. The great object of the discipline which he undergoes is to make him what is called "a good prisoner," which means an automaton who obeys arbitrary rules, and this necessarily diminishes rather than cultivates his power of self-reliance and independent action. He is placed almost exclusively under the charge of warders, and, unless he commits some offence against the prison code, scarcely ever comes under the eye of the governor; and these warders are selected from a class of men especially unfit for the discharge of the functions which are entrusted to them. Sir Joshua Jebb obstinately persists in conferring these appointments upon old soldiers; and their fitness for the duty may be judged of from the fact that out of the inferior body of officers at Chatham prison, numbering not more than 100 men, there have been dismissed for neglect of duty and insubordination, since the opening of the prison four years ago, no less than fifty-four, besides compulsory resignations; and sixteen of these were discharged for drunkenness on duty. Such are a few of the charges brought against our convict system not by a speculative philanthropist, but by a practical man who has had considerable experience in directing the organization which he condemns. In the face of such accusations it is impossible that the Government can refuse a public and impartial inquiry. It is easy enough to denounce these men as "incarnate fiends," and to clamour for the infliction upon them of severe retribution for their revolt. For our own part, we regard them with no feelings of sentimental compassion. But we cannot forget that most of them will some day return to society as free men; and if it be true, as we believe it is, that the training which they are now undergoing has a positive tendency to make them worse, instead of better, it is obvious that so pernicious a state of things should be put an end to without delay. The public have a right to know whether their money is spent in nurturing the evil tendencies of those whom penal discipline should strive to cure; and the truth can be elicited, not by an inquiry with closed doors, conducted by the parties who are impeached, and resulting only in the flogging, and chaining together, and exposure, and solitary confinement on bread and water, of those whom they are accused of injuring, but by an open investigation, at which both the parties concerned shall have a fair hearing.—*Star and Dial.*

CONCLUSION.

MY LORDS AND GENTLEMEN—Enough has been adduced to prove that much remains to follow. That the system is rotten you cannot fail to see; that Sir Joshua Jebb is totally unfitted for his office must be apparent, if the foregoing is true. To give Sir Joshua Jebb a chance to clear his system of all the charges I have now made against it, your Honourable House of Parliament will deem it right to have a *public* and *most searching* inquiry. Such has been my sole object in this letter; because I know that if the matters I here adduce receive that public attention which they deserve and demand, then will abuses get reformed—convicts receive judicious and reformatory training, and I and others—the cruelly-used victims of Sir Joshua Jebb and his system — will receive that justice from the hands of the country, which, as long as he is permitted to go on in secret, upheld by the apathy and sheltering indifference of successive Home Secretaries, it is useless to expect. It is painful to have thus to write of a public man; and even more so when that public man has the reputation of a Philanthropist, a Prison Reformer, and Christian; but stern truth and inflexible justice require that the flimsy veil which man may succeed in throwing over his own system should, when the innocent suffer, or the country bleeds, be cast aside. In the interest, the temporal and eternal interest, of 10,000 imprisoned convicts I write; and on the behalf of upwards of 1,000 terror-ruled officers, I have drawn from the dark secrets of our English convict system, that impenetrable veil which Sir Joshua Jebb, by his partial Blue Books, has managed for years to uphold.

I feel that I have discharged my conscience; it now remains for Parliament and the country to take the matter up—being ready when called upon to appear before any public tribunal, and prove the facts adduced in this letter.

Those that know me best, know that my earnest effort has been to benefit my fellow-men. This effort must, with the blessing of God, have that effect. I shall be content to know, that for three years I have suffered privation and often severe distress, because, in the cause of my fellow-men, even though the offscouring of the earth, I dared to offend my superiors in revealing solemn though most shocking truths.

I have the honour to remain,
Your Lordships' and Gentlemen of Her Majesty's Commons'
Most obedient, humble Servant,
WILLIAM THWAITES,
LAY AGENT,
Late First Schoolmaster in Her Majesty's Convict Prisons.

APPENDIX.

Official letters between Sir J. Jebb, Sir G. Grey, and Mr. Waddington on the one hand, and the Rev. J. K. Walpole on the other, published in a letter to Sir G. Grey by Mr. Walpole in 1859.

Stirling Castle Hulk, Gosport, March 20, 1856.

Sir,—I beg permission to address you, and to state with what pain I view the approaching execution on Saturday next, the 22nd, of the sentence passed on Thomas Jones, for the murder of Mr. Hope.

I could not, of course, presume to offer a remark on the subject had things been conducted here as they ought to have been.

On myself personally, and in the discharge of my duties they have operated severely enough ; but I have never, hitherto, had any hopes of obtaining redress.

The investigation of the Commissioners sent by you, having discovered such a previous state of disorganization and demoralization among the prisoners—the place was actually not a prison—and abuses having reached that height, where nothing of the sort ought to have existed, had all done their duty, that it was only what might have been expected, that prisoners, according to their abnormal code of thinking, should have meditated evil. This passing on from stage to stage has resulted in the dreadful catastrophe.

Under all circumstances, I cannot help thinking that the execution of the convict will be pointed at as a sad comment upon an ill-conducted establishment subject to your control ; and I would most humbly submit, that, if it should seem good to you, the sentence should be commuted to imprisonment for life.

I think it possible, that from your better experience and qualifications for deciding on the question, you may take a different view from the one I do ; yet I would beseech you to ascribe to me only proper motives in making this representation, and considering that the life of a man is concerned.

I am, Sir, your obedient servant,
(Signed)   J. K. WALPOLE, Chaplain.

The Right Honourable Sir George Grey, &c., &c., &c.

2, 4, 56.   J. S.   45, Parliament Street, 1st April, 1856.

Sir,—I have received a letter from Mr. Waddington, dated the 31st ultimo, from which the following is an extract :

" I could not, of course, presume to offer a remark on the subject, had things been conducted here as they ought to have been—on myself personally, and in the discharge of my duties, they have operated severely enough ; but I have never hitherto had any hopes of obtaining redress.

" The investigation of the commissioners sent by you having discovered such a previous state of disorganization and demoralization among the prisoners—the place was actually not a prison—and abuses having reached that height, where nothing of the sort ought to have existed had all done their duty, that it was only what might be expected, that prisoners, according to their abnormal kind of thinking, should have meditated evil. This passing on from stage to stage, has resulted in the dreadful catastrophe."

Sir George Grey desires that the chaplain may be informed that it was his duty not to have allowed the disorganization and demoralization among the prisoners to which he adverts to have existed, without having called the attention of the directors, and through them of the Secretary of State, to evils of such magnitude as these which he describes ; and that he may be called upon to account for this obvious neglect of duty, and to state more particularly the nature of the misconduct which his letter imputes to the officers in charge of the hulk. Sir George Grey is the more surprised that this should be the first intimation given by Mr. Walpole of the existence of such evils, as on reference to his reports, the general tenor of them appears to be calculated to produce a very different impression. He adverts, no doubt, to the inherent defects of a hulk establishment, as compared with a prison on shore ; but in the extract given from his report in the General Report on Convict Prisons for 1853, he notices the vigilance and exertions both of discipline and educational officers, as producing effects that agreeably surprise, under the unfavourable condition of things, arising from the prisoners being confined in a hulk ; and there is nothing either in that or his subsequent report, implying an opinion that the conduct of the officers was open to reprehension, or that the conduct of the prisoners was bad ; much less that there was a state of disorganization and demoralization attributable, as appears now to be his opinion, to the neglect of duty on the part of the officers, which resulted in the murder of Mr. Hope.

In accordance with Sir George Grey's wishes, I have to call upon you first, to account for the neglect of duty referred to, and, secondly, that you will state more particularly the nature of the misconduct which you impute to officers in charge of the *Stirling Castle* and *Briton* hulks.

I am, Sir, your obedient servant,
(Signed)   J. JEBB, Col.

Rev. J. K. Walpole, *Stirling Castle* Hulk.

Copy of memorandum which accompanied the preceding letter.

The enclosed letter for the Rev. Mr. Walpole is sent to the Governor for his perusal, after which it is requested that it may be handed to Mr. Walpole.

45 Parliament Street, 1st April, 1856.

The enclosed is forwarded for the chaplain as directed.

J. SHAW, Governor.

2, 4, 56. J. K. W., 2, 4, 56.   (This memo. to be returned.)

On the 3*rd December*, 1856, *nine* days before I *was* dismissed, Colonel Jebb addressed to me a purposely adapted letter, which he sent *under cover*, *to the Governor, Captain Warren*, for *him* first to read and *copy*, after which to hand to me what was my own *private* property. I have Captain Warren's note, which he sent me with the letter, and of which the following is a copy :—

Defence, 4th December, 1856.

SIR,—I beg to forward the accompanying letter from Colonel Jebb, which I have perused according to his instructions.

I have the honour to be, Sir, your obedient servant,
(Signed)   J. S. WARREN.

Was this again proper treatment of a clergyman, sir, or indeed of the humblest individual ? How, sir, *could* you have sanctioned it ? You remember, sir, that in the course of the correspondence, in striving to avert my ruin, I continually appealed to you, *imploring* your protection, which was in fact the Queen's protection, and which, with the most devoted love and loyalty to her Majesty, I knew to be no fiction.

Well, sir, on the afternoon of the 12*th December*, 1856, when I had just returned from visiting the convicts in the punishment cells, Captain Gambier, the visiting director, was announced. and I received him in the chaplain's office. He then handed me a letter from Colonel Jebb to myself of that day's date, which I found on opening to contain my *instant* dismissal. The following extract will suffice for the present :—

"I have now to inform you, that having consulted my colleagues (Captain O'Brien and Captain Gambier), we are unanimously of opinion that it is a duty to look to the public interests, and that they cannot fail to be prejudiced by the continuance of any one in the execution of the important duties of chaplain, who *has given the superior officers of the ship so many and such just causes of offence.*—We are, THEREFORE, of opinion that it will be most for the interests of the service to make temporary provision for the discharge of these duties, and to release you from further attendance and responsibility."

The above, sir, shows the reason *assigned* for my dismissal. The old charge contained in Colonel Jebb's letter of April 1, 1856, *had been abandoned*, and as may be seen in this letter, a new, extemporized, and *vague* one was announced, and acted upon without a moment's delay.

Captain Gambier knew that there was not the slightest shadow of truth in this charge. I never heard it breathed until I read it in this letter ; no officers who may have accused me of offending them, had ever been brought face to face with me. This was Captain Gambier's duty as visiting directer, to have done, sir, had all been *bona fide*. But it had that morning been settled in a *private* conference in London that I was to be dismissed. I was utterly in the dark, sir, as to what was going on against me from first to last. That Captain O'Brien should have given his voice towards my dismissal, I am greatly astonished, as he knew that his duties prevented him from having any acquaintance whatever with the proceedings in the Hulks.

The *intention* of Colonel Jebb in sending my letter *through Captain Warren* may now be seen, sir, viz., that as I was to be accused of "offending the officers," Captain Warren, the governor's aid was indispensable to establish this point. It is with the greatest pain I state, sir, that on the *3rd November*, just one month *before* Captain Warren received my letter from Colonel Jebb, he had sent to Captain Gambier, the visiting director, a wilfully false charge against me, that I had neglected my duties, and which caused me to occupy my time in a correspondence with Captain O'Brien and Captain Gambier, and which, sir, you may see in Colonel Jebb's office. In about three weeks, sir, this charge was quite abandoned.

I can allude only briefly, sir, to the *reasons* which have been assigned for my dismissal since it took place, by saying that the variety has been perfectly astounding. Mr. Roebuck, M.P., in 1857 ; Sir Charles Napier, M.P., in 1858 ; and Mr. Angerstein, M.P., in 1859 ; all three received different answers in the business.

An influential clergyman also, who interested himself greatly on my behalf, was informed, sir, by you, in writing, that Colonel Jebb was so urgent for my dismissal, that you had no alternative left—while Colonel Jebb assured the same clergyman, that he had used every effort to induce you not to dismiss me, but that you would not listen to him. Sir, "*Quo teneam vultus mutantem Protea nodo ?*" one cannot help exclaiming, under the sense of such insult added to injury.

I must also notice the very cruel and groundless calumnies which have been circulated, as I have found *broadcast through England*, to my injury—another proof that I did not deserve to be dismissed, and the object of which has been to *attempt* to account for my dismissal, the *assigned* reason in Colonel Jebb's letter of December 12th, 1856, having actually been *denied* to my friends to have been the reason, and which Colonel Jebb himself has also denied to me, in writing, to have been the reason. Really, sir, the English of the present day is not intelligible. Of course, sir, the reason *assigned* in Colonel Jebb's letter of Dec. 12th, was not the real reason ; and you know, sir, there was no just reason at all why I should have been dismissed. But I have reminded you, sir, in what my dismissal *originated*, as shown by my interpretation of the united letter of April 1st, 1856.

It must suffice to give one specimen of the calumnies, viz., that my "temper was so violent, that none of the convict officers could or would work with me ;" an assertion which numerous friends know from my *universal* manners and temper to be *without a shadow of truth*. All the others are equally groundless. Had these really existed, is it not unaccountable, sir, that they are *not mentioned* in the correspondence which took place.

It remains yet to be explained, sir, why pains were taken successfully to cut me off from an appointment which I was hoping to receive in the summer of 1857, while you were still in office, and which was totally unconnected with your department.

I had written thus far, sir, when I received by post, a copy of Major Stewart's (late deputy-governor of Chatham prison) letter to Sir Joshua Jebb, printed by Horsey, Queen Street, Portsea, and I find that Major Stewart has been treated by Colonel Jebb and Captain Gambier, in the same unprincipled and perfidious way that I was—to the loss of his appointment. Major Stewart says, page 10 :— "You must be also aware that I am not the only person you have maligned in this manner. But it is quite consistent with yourself, when a man is dismissed, or passed over by the promotion of others to remark :—

"He is quarrelsome, injudicious, indiscreet, troublesome, or has lost influence with the officers and prisoners."

Very vague and general charges, which would not be worth notice, did they not furnish you with a weapon wherewith to inflict wounds upon your unfortunate victims.

It is truly shocking sir, to see one officer after another sacrificed with his family to a corporation as secret and cruel as "the Holy Office." So cruel, sir, is the tyranny of Colonel Jebb's prison system, that an officer still in her Majesty's convict service described it in a letter to a friend not long since, as "the French Empire in miniature," which was suggested to him from his own sufferings.

I cannot omit, sir, to notice the dismissal of Mr. Thwaites, head schoolmaster in the establishment in which I was chaplain, when he was within a few weeks of being due for his retiring pension. It was a result of the same " commission." You dismissed him in reality, sir, *because* he supplied such amazing facts in evidence to your commissioners on their requisition. Without him they could never have come at the real truth of the dark depths they *discovered*—that is, the Queen discovered through them, what it behoved her Majesty, yourself, sir, and the public to know. Mr. Thwaites's attention had been first directed to his facts by some *employé* of the public contractors. *I have personal knowledge*, sir, that he was fairly hunted to death by Colonel Jebb, through the instrumentality of Captain Gambier, visiting director, and Captain Warren, the governor of Lewes prison. That Mr. Thwaites's dismissal should have been the result of charges against Captain Warren, heard before Mr. Hall, of Bow Street, by your direction, is about the most astonishing of all results. I was summoned, sir, to give evidence on that inquiry, and knowing all the evidence, I and many more am astonished at the result. There are other officers likewise unjustly dismissed sir, who are not able to make their cry for mercy heard.

Copy of Sir George Grey's Reply to the Rev. J. K. Walpole's "Letter," of December 6th, 1859.

Eaton Place, December 10th, 1859.

Sir,—I beg to acknowledge the receipt of your letter of the 6th inst., which reached me only this day. While I sincerely regret the painful circumstances in which you inform me that you and your family have been placed, I must remind you of what I said to you in answer to a former letter which I received from you (in the time if I remember right of my immediate successor at the Home Office), that any representation you desire to make with reference to your removal from the office you held in the public service should be addressed to the Secretary of State for the Home Department, who has the means from the documents in his office of forming his opinion as to the reasons for that removal.

I am, Sir, your obedient servant,

The Rev. J. K. Walpole. (Signed) G. GREY.

Copy of the Rev. J. K. Walpole's answer to Sir George Grey's reply of the 10th December, 1859.

Brighton, December 13th, 1859.

Sir,—I beg to acknowledge the receipt (yesterday) of your note of the 10th inst. in acknowledgement of my letter to you of the 6th inst. The reason that received it only on the 10th, was that I posted it here on that morning.

I thank you, Sir, for saying :—" I sincerely regret the painful circumstances in which you inform me that you and your family have been placed ;" but, Sir, I beg leave to offer a remark on what you immediately follow on with :—

G

"I must remind you of what I said to you in answer to a former letter which I received from you (in the time if I remember right of my immediate successor at the Home Office) that any representation you desire to make with reference to your removal from the office you held in the public service should be addressed to the Secretary of State for the Home Department, who has the means from the documents in his office of forming his opinion as to the reasons for that removal."

Mr. Walpole was your successor, Sir, at the Home Office, and I did address him on my business, when the result was, that I received an answer from Mr. Waddington, by direction of Mr. Secretary Walpole, which concluded by informing me, that as you (his predecessor) had settled the question, he could not re-open it, and finally begging to decline any further correspondence on the subject. You may suppose, Sir, from this time, that it is never my intention again to address the Home Secretary on my business.

This being the case, Sir, I would respectfully request you to consider in what way you intend to provide for me, in reparation of the incredibly unjust and cruel treatment I have received at your hands, and which you find described, and *traced to its source*, in my letter to you of the 6th inst., and which, Sir, you admit by your silence on it.

Allow me to remind you, Sir, that you, and you only, are responsible for the very unjust treatment I have received.

I would beg of you, Sir, to favour me with an immediate answer.

I am, Sir, your very obedient and respectful servant,
                                        J. K. WALPOLE.
                            Late Chaplain in her Majesty's Convict Service.
The Right Honourable Sir George Grey, Bart., M.P., &c.

Copy of Sir George Grey's reply to the Rev. J. K. Walpole's letter of the 13th inst. :—
                                        London, December 16, 1859.
Sir,—I must decline any further correspondence with you on the subject of your removal from the public service.
                            I am, Sir, your obedient servant,
The Rev. J. K. Walpole.   (Signed)   G. GREY.

Copy of the Rev. J. K. Walpole's answer to Sir George Grey's reply of December 16, 1859 :—
                    Brighton, Tuesday Evening, December 20, 1859.
Sir,—I have received your note of the 16th inst., on Saturday, the 17th, and allow me, Sir, to say that I deeply regret to find it so unsatisfactory.

You decline, Sir, to hold any further correspondence with me on my "removal (more properly dismissal) from the public service." Will you permit me, sir, to remind you, with the deepest respect and pain, that as her Majesty's Home Secretary of State, you should never have sanctioned the *commencement* of the unjust and cruel correspondence on the 1st of April, 1856, and which was *intended*, as I have shown you, to lead to my ruin. I have offered you a full explanation of that united letter of April 1st, and its consequences, in my letter to you of the 6th inst.

I cannot make any further communication to you, Sir, on the subject ; and I have informed you that the place of appeal to which you yourself directed me in your letter of the 10th, is closed against me.

My case, Sir, is urgent—the sufferings of my family are past physical endurance, as you know from my letter of the 6th.

You may suppose, Sir, that after more than three years of suffering, and at this inclement season, I must seek to find whether Christian England does not contain some source whence a conclusion may be found to the punishment of my wife and children.   I am, Sir, as ever,
                    Your very obedient and respectful servant,
                                        J. K. WALPOLE,
                            Late Chaplain in her Majesty's Convict Service.
The Right Honourable Sir George Grey, Bart., M.P., &c., &c., &c.

The facts contained in the preceding five letters, and the tenor of the letters, on either side, require no comment ; they speak for themselves. With the most inexpressible grief and reluctance these letters are now committed to print, the responsibility of which proceeding resting elsewhere than with

J. K. WALPOLE,

Late Chaplain in her Majesty's Convict Service.

Brighton, December 27th, 1859.

Attempted suicide of a warder.—Showing the state of Chatham Prison in 1857.

"ATTEMPTED SUICIDE.—A few days since, a warder of convicts, named Fraser, late of the *Warrior* hulk, Woolwich, and since employed at the new convict prison at Chatham, was discovered lying upon the grave of his first wife, at Plumstead, with his throat cut in a most fearful manner. The reason assigned by the unhappy man for this desperate attempt on his life is, that he was informed . by Captain —— that he was to be dismissed the convict service at the end of the month, for having been overheard in a conversation with his brother officer, to say something that was considered to reflect upon the governor of Chatham prison. Fraser further stated that he believed a fixed intention existed to single out all the warders who had served in the hulks, and dismiss or drive them from the service, and that, after having performed his duties as convict warder for more than fifteen years without a stain upon his character, the idea of dismissal without any just grounds was more than he could bear. The correspondent who forwards us an account of the occurrence considers that the statement of the warder demands inquiry on the part of Sir George Grey, and that the sooner he investigates the management of the convict prison at Chatham the better, more especially as strange rumours are afloat concerning the system pursued in that establishment. Fraser still lies dangerously ill at Plumstead, whither he was removed after the suicidal act." [This officer was restored to his office when he recovered].—*Daily Telegraph*, April 6th, 1857.

The following letter from Sir Joshua Jebb is inserted in the appendix to show that I sought his protection in vain—and well I might, when I sought it from the very men whom he had privately instructed against me.

(Copy.)   45 Parliament Street, 5 May, 1857.

SIR,—I have to acknowledge the receipt of your letter of the 4th instant, stating that in seeking an interview, you did so to obtain my protection, as you have known that for some months that there were certain persons who sought your destruction ; that you were willing to write, but must first receive from me an assurance that you shall not be injured by giving information of an unpleasant character.

In reply, I beg to say that I can enter into no compromise or agreement of any kind with you.

If you bring forward any evidence calculated to establish the fact you insinuate, a full investigation shall be made, and the parties concerned will take the consequences.

I am, Sir, your obedient servant,

J. JEBB.

I did not write, as if I had my written statement would have been shown to those concerned, their simple answer would have been asked, that would have been all the investigation, and I should only have had my dismissal some months earlier than I did.

The following letters will prove that it was not my fault the convict service abuses were not thorougly sifted and exposed by a Parliamentary Committee before which I was examined in the year 1856.

(Copy, verbatim.)   106 High Street, Gosport, 17 June, 1856.

SIR,—In giving my evidence the other day I omitted to mention a most material feature, which acts most detrimentally against the reformation of convicts, and if this is not an irregular proceeding, I beg to offer this paper as evidence.

I have observed during the last eight years, that a most immoral selection of men has been made to act as the governors and superior officers in the convict prisons. I have acted with two governors who have embezzled the public money, and who were very immoral openly; I have also acted with two others who were discharged for improper conduct. The other superior officers many of them were licentious and openly profane. Swearing at convicts has been carried on to a most fearful extent. The inferior officers have many of them been selected from the army; and as a class they are the worst possible to have the management of criminals. They are most of them addicted to swearing, in fact I have seen that little hope can be held of the *reformation* of criminals until more care is bestowed upon selecting fit, moral, and judicious men to act as officers over them.

I have also to mention that I have known schoolmasters selected who could not, from the want of attainments, give moral and religious instruction to criminals.

I will here also mention that the officers who have the control of convicts, are dissatisfied with the way promotion is given, and while they are dissatisfied men, your system cannot work well.

Lastly, *I must state that the inspection of hulks and prisons, as I have experienced, is not what it ought to be to prevent abuses and the growth of vice among convicts and officers.*

Prison directors should visit hulks and prisons unexpectedly; they should allow men of integrity an opportunity to point out what they had observed; in a word—at present, it is possible for the most fearful abuses to exist, and the prison directors be ignorant of them. Such was the case in this ship until I pointed them out to a commission from the crown.

I remain, Sir, your obedient servant,

WM. THWAITES.

To the Right Hon. M. T. Baines, Esq., M.P.,
Chairman of Committee on Transportation.

The following is the answer :— .

House of Commons, June 23, 1856.

Sir,—I have submitted to the committee on transportation your letter of the 17th instant, with regard to the unfitness of the present officers exercising a salutary control over convicts, and also with regard to the system of promotion among the officers, and the laxity of inspection on the part of the prison directors. The committee direct me to say that, *although they are all points of great importance,* they think your proper course will be, instead of laying them before this committee, by whom they could not be satisfactorily investigated, to lay the facts before the Secretary of State for the Home Department, who has it in his power to direct a full and searching inquiry, by means of which the truth may be ascertained, and justice done to all parties.

I remain, yours faithfully,

Mr. Thwaites.
M. T. BAINES.

I need not say that I did not write to Sir G. Grey, inasmuch as I had given his commissioners all the information the March preceding, and the result is known by the pages of this pamphlet. The guilty were shielded, and the innocent, who gave the "points of great importance," have been hunted from the service.

Need I ask is government inquiry a farce or perversion of justice? When secret, it is worse than farce, it is positive atrocity. Open, public inquiry alone can stem the tide of abuse now raging in the convict service.

www.ingramcontent.com/pod-product-compliance
Lightning Source LLC
Chambersburg PA
CBHW031452270326
41930CB00007B/965